Feb 21, 1999

To ... and yours, Sincerely, ...uardi

MARIA
BELLA

by

Austin Goodrich

Published by Thistlefield Studio
Printed by Network Printers
Milwaukee, Wisconsin

MARIA BELLA

Published by:
Thistlefield Studio
Franklin, WI 53132-9657

ISBN 0-9664172-C-8

Library of Congress
Catalog Card Number:
98-60793

Acknowledgment

Thank you, John Suardi, for your friendship, encouragement and lucid recall, without which this book could never have been writ.

A special thanks to John Bergera for his research on life in the area of Spring Valley, Illinois.

Thanks to Mona Goodrich for her cover design and her patience.

To Mona and Samantha

with love.

CHAPTER 1

Young women with shining faces scurried about the house chirping continuously in the manner of newborn chicks. Old women with faces lined by disillusionment and work in the fields moved about only as much as needed to do the things that needed to be done in preparing the wedding of Maria Roscio.

The bride sat silently by the window as her mother, Giovanna, put the finishing touches to the neckline of a wedding dress that she wore twenty years before and had now reconstructed to fit her daughter's petite dimensions. As she put in the final stitch, Signora Roscio looked at her spotted and calloused hands and then at the soft white hands of her daughter and nodded with approval. Her daughter, her only child, sole object of love that could have nourished a dozen children had the birth been less complicated, was to be married. She was ready, and Giovanna with well-deserved pride, took most of the credit. Although her husband, Orenzo

Boggio Roscio, had been a devoted father, long hours of laying brick and stone left him with little energy for the needs of his family beyond the considerable job of putting bread and wine on the family table.

Signora Roscio often returned from the fields to read to her daughter until the two of them fell into a warm slumber together. It was Mama who taught Maria to build her life on the solid rock of the Church and abide by the lessons of the catechism. And it was Mama who taught her the social graces – proper posture, speaking in a polite manner, eating with cutlery – that escaped most of the working class children in the village.

Giovanna looked down at Maria's hands, folded decorously in front of the breasts that stretched the lacey bodice of her gown. It was as if all of the quality instilled in Maria during her sixteen years on earth could be seen in these delicate hands and the temple of innocence they were poised to protect.

"Well, what do you think?"

"About what, Mama?"

Maria blushed. She was afraid that she had not been thinking of things she should have been thinking about. Looking out the open window, Maria's thoughts were far from her wedding. Up in the cool, clean air of the mountains beyond the village, sheep grazed as if painted on the lush green canvas of grass. Surely they were there to give the landscape a living touch, she thought, to soften the rough ridges of gray bedrock that stretched all the way up into the snow that wrapped the majestic peak of Mount Blanc.

"Why, your dress, silly girl. What do you think of your dress."

"I love it, Mama. It's the most beautiful dress in the world. It's wonderful."

"I'm so glad you like it," whispered Giovanna. "Come, let's take a look in the mirror." As Maria turned to the full length mirror that stood in the middle of the bedroom, she took a hand mirror to view the back of the dress and fix her hairdo. She saw the gorgeous scenery reflected in the mirror.

"Oh, Mama, the dress is perfect and just look out the window."

"What?"

"Look, it's so clear you can see Mount Blanc. And feel that fresh air, the breeze moving the lace on the curtain – and on my dress – it's all so perfect." As she said this, the real significance of the day struck Maria and the smile slid off her face. Giovanna sensed her daughter's distress and held out her arms to take her baby into her embrace.

"It is perfect, isn't it Mama?"

As she moved to her mother, the mirror dropped from her hand and smashed on the marble floor. Maria was startled and looked down in frozen terror as an aunt, whose crippled ankle caused her to walk in a strange manner, tried to console her. As she clumsily swept up the splinters, her mother's older sister said, "It's nothing to worry about, Maria."

"But this portends bad luck, isn't it so?"

"No, dear child, that's just a crazy old superstition. Something that unhappy people who don't like to take responsibility for their lives use to explain the cause of their unhappiness." Auntie Gina began to laugh, some-what hysterically, and was joined by two bridesmaids who were drawn into the room by the sound of breaking glass.

Giovanna Boggio Roscio did not join in the laughter. She believed in the bad omen of the broken looking glass, as she believed in all of the thousands of similar superstitions held so closely by the men and women of her age. She know that they too often came true. She remembered how a black cat had run across the street when she was walking to school with Gina, and how the wheel of a hay wagon drawn by an obstreperous donkey had crushed her sister's foot a few minutes later. Giovanna's terrible instant recollection ended abruptly as a dark cloud swept the horizon, blotting out the mountain and casting an ominous shadow into the room. This supernatural sign combined with the broken mirror to produce a chill that ran visibly through the prematurely bent body of the mother of the bride. "I should have known," she whispered to herself.

She had been anxious about the possibility of her beloved daughter finding happiness with Antonio Vallero, and the feeling was worsened by a wrenching sense of guilt; for Giovanna had agreed to an arranged marriage promoted mainly by the groom's family. It seems that all of their efforts to find a suitable woman of his own standing – the son of a well-to-do merchant – had failed. In plain language, they were told that no self-respecting woman would ever marry Antonio Vallero. Giovanna had agreed to the union because of a deep conviction grounded in her own experience that the marriage would give her daughter a chance to move up several rungs on the ladder of social respectability to a higher class, to preserve those lovely white hands for playing cards or playing the piano, but never for picking olives or grapes.

Just then the sound of breaking furniture stormed into the bedroom through the open window from the direction of the cafe just two doors down the street. A falling table served as the prelude to a cacophony of broken glass. A stern rebuke followed in its wake:

"Get up, Antonio. You're getting married today, you asshole, *i ze prope un faso!*"

It was the voice of Maria's father, comparing his future son-in-law to a bean.

❖❖❖

As she walked up the steps to the entrance of the church, Maria felt as if she were playing the lead role in a dream that should have been happy but was strangely, ominously distressing. The sudden realization of her unhappiness produced a shudder that flowed into the strong arm of her father, who looked down at his daughter with a forced smile of reassurance. The Church of Saint Augustine had always been associated with happy, or, at worst, emotionally neutral occasions. Maria had been christened there as an infant and had seen herself in a long lacey gown in a grey tintype photo that was pulled out and shown visitors whenever they showed any sign of interest in her. She had received confirmation at the altar of Saint Augustine, only, it seemed to her, a few days ago. The church's sunbaked white walls on the outside offered a surprising contrast with the cool comfort of its sanctuary. It was always a place of solitude, of escape from the heat of living into the cool tranquility of a promised afterlife. It was a place that Maria loved: for the thrill of union with the supernatural through Holy Communion and the liberating joy provided by the nervous release of guilt in the dank, mahagony walls of the confessional.

Today, none of her past happiness entered her thoughts. Nor could past memories be conjured up to blot out the questions that dominated her consciousness. What am I doing here? Why should my marriage to a rich man seem like a bad dream? But then, the realization struck Maria that dreams – even childhood imaginings of a happy marriage of love shared with a prince – could never be chosen or summoned into existence. Like the weather, dreams just happen in forms of their own seemingly, capricious choosing. And Maria glanced up to see a curtain of dark clouds closing across the horizon. She then moved her gaze up to the weather-beaten face of her father, which testified to his work outdoors. A smile shaped her ample lips that looked rosy against her unusually fair skin. And she suddenly felt the need to comfort him.

"Ciao, Papa," Maria whispered.

"Ciao, bambina mia." Orenzo Boggio Roscio gazed down at the grown woman who would always be his baby daughter. And he patted the tiny hand that held his arm with a surprisingly firm grip. Maria started to lower her gaze to his hand but quickly looked back into her papa's face, knowing that he usually kept his right hand in his pocket or behind his back to conceal the mutilated thumb that had been smashed by a sledge hammer as he held a fence post. It was an accident he had told Maria with a tone of finality that precluded further discussion. But town talk that reached her ears only recently whispered that the sledge hammer was swung by an outraged suitor, who had asked for Maria's hand in marriage and had been turned down by Orenzo.

Maria's dark premonition returned as she reached the altar and, after a searching look at her father, forced herself to break away from him to receive the holy sacrament of marriage. Beside her was her husband-to-be. Forever, thought Maria, with an abbreviated prayer for divine intercession: oh, dear God, please ... Antonio Vallero was swaying slightly as he looked at his bride through rheumy eyes filled with lust. The sweet-sour smell of wine seemed to come from every pore of his body. She considered running from the church, of running until some compassionate soul would take pity on her and provide asylum. But she was forced to cut short this escape fantasy by the sudden realization that wherever she went, she would always encounter herself. Maria Roscio would be there to greet her, to admonish her for betraying not just her betrothed, but her loving parents and the Church in which her life was vested.

The couple knelt to receive their blessing delivered by the stern-faced Father Pietro, a church official from Torino who sometimes presided at important affairs such as this wedding involving as it did the son of one of the church's more generous benefactors. The old parish priest, Father John, was said to be at home in bed with a head cold. Maria missed him, but was secretly glad that his absence would spare her the indignity of making fraudulent promises in the presence of a man who knew her as well or better than she knew herself.

"I now pronounce you man and wife," intoned the priest, looking straight into the eyes of Maria in a way that sent a chill down her spine. When he licked his lips before telling the groom that he could now kiss the bride, Maria got a queasy feeling about Father Pietro of the Torino office.

Facing the assembled guests Maria, for the first time, was struck with their contrasting appearances. On one side of the aisle were her neighbors and friends, simple people dressed in their finest Sunday attire. The men had on their baggy black suits, the only matching jacket and trousers in their sparse wardrobes. No neckties. The women's clothes seemed to be cut from the same bolt of fabric, differentiated only by brightly-colored sashes and scarves. Their heads were covered by large tasseled bandannas, most of them white. No powder was used to disguise the fact that many of them spent most of their time working in the bright sunshine that bathed the rocky countryside near the French border in the region of Valle D'Aosta.

On the other side of the aisle sat the groom's family and friends. There were only a third as many of them, but the variety and quality of their clothes made up for their lack of numbers. The men wore tailored worsted suits in grey and herringbone tweeds. Their ties were hand-tied and made of the finest silk, sometimes with matching pocket handkerchiefs. The women wore brightly-colored dresses of satin and chiffon that fit as only the work of skilled seamstresses can fit, without appearing to be professionally tailored. Their fashionably coiffed heads were covered by hats of pure silk or satin sewn by hand.

The scene in this little northern Italian sanctuary was a perfect microcosmic caricature of the class struggle that Karl Marx had posited as the political cornerstone of his theory and that Lenin was busily transforming into a prescription for seizing and holding onto political power. The newly unified and independent country of Italy was just beginning to experience the human dynamics that led to socialism and its nationalist spin-off, fascism.

Maria left church as she had entered it: in a state of confusion tinged with sadness. Only a thumbs up signal from her mother brought a smile to her face as she marched outside. The smile broadened as the strains of festive music reached her from the town square.

"Oh, Antonio, listen. Is that music being played for us?"

"Of course it's for us, you and me, just the two of us," said Antonio, "and about a thousand villagers."

Determined to enjoy her wedding reception at all costs, Maria parried the sarcastic thrust of the remark and went on: "Come along, my blushing groom, let's dance!" As the violinist and accordion player struck up a waltz, she took Antonio by the hand and started to dance. He responded by kissing her shoulder and throat.

After a few clumsy steps, Antonio broke loose and headed for one of the tables surrounding the square holding several bottles of wine, shouting over his shoulder to his bride: "have fun, my lovely wife, have fun!"

Rescued by her father, Maria was whisked around the open square in perfect step to the increasingly fast tempo set by the musicians. At the end of the waltz,

Maria and her father collapsed into chairs, laughing, and she caught the eye of the accordion player who returned her glance with an entranced smile. All of the men, it seemed, wanted to dance with the bride and as she got caught up in the music, singing and laughter, she began to believe that perhaps, after all, she might have been a happy marriage. And why not? With all the happiness in the air, surely there must be enough to go around. "Joy," she shouted, and threw her arms into the cooling night air.

At that very moment, the air was rent with the sound of crashing woodwork and glass, as Antonio Vallero fell down and pulled a table with him. Maria's smile vanished and then slowly returned as her eyes were drawn to the musician. He looked at her with something more than compassion, as he began to sing the lively *Tic-Toc Polka*, a song designed to recapture her happy mood. They would, she knew, meet again.

CHAPTER 2

In the spring of 1910, Maria was eighteen years old and in labor with her first child.She had wanted to have the baby at home, where her mother could be near her and she would be surrounded with the pictures, furniture, and goosedown comforter and coffee cups she had grown to love during the first year of a loveless marriage. As she felt her time approaching, Maria made a final plea to have her baby at home.

Antonio Vallero, her husband, would not hear of it. "Having babies at home is for peasants," he had sneered. "The only reason they do it is that they can't afford to pay for a hospital room and proper modern medical care." Knowing full well that he was talking about his beautiful wife's people, whom she loved as she would never love him, he continued. "Why, hell, they couldn't make a down payment on a bedpan."

Antonio Vallero's raucous laughter filled the three

rooms of their neatly if sparsely furnished bungalow. The low ceilings, mottled by the stains of kerosene lamp smoke, produced an echo effect that seemed to amplify the rude sound as it passed out the bedroom window into the vineyards that stretched northward to the French Alps. Maria moved to the window to survey a scene that always healed the wounds inflicted by her husband.

The rushing waters of a mountain stream produced a rhapsody as they kicked and churned their way under an old wooden bridge that had survived several decades of spring floods by the narrowest of margins and would soon be put to the test again. Tongues of water were already licking the bottom of the bridge and the more cautious of the villagers took a kilometer detour to drive their oxen-drawn carts over the steel bridge in the center of town.

Clusters of daffodils and crocuses couldn't wait to show their exuberant colors and were sprouting up through the last patches of ice-crusted snow. As was her custom when living with her mama and papa, Maria loved to plant the bulbs each autumn in a random arrangement so that her gardens would be full of surprises in the spring. "How dull it would be," she had explained, "if you were to know exactly where each flower and each color would appear. Why, this would take all of the suspense and excitement out of planting a garden in the first place."

The first pain was like a mild stomach cramp, a case of indigestion caused by eating too much Pasticcio di Maccheroni. Maria continued to stand by the open window. Her husband had already left for an evening of wine and cards with his cronies at the corner cafe. "Let me know if anything should happen," he called out as he left the house. Maria was a week overdue and Vallero acted as if the delay was a deliberate move on her part to disrupt his life and gain sympathy for herself.

Then the pain became deeper, longer-lasting and at regular intervals. In the middle of a serious cramp, Maria forced herself to stand erect, take a deep breath, and feast her eyes on the beauty of her landscape, which had suddenly darkened after the sun slipped behind the mountains. She walked the six blocks to the hospital, taking a small detour around the last block to avoid the possibility of her husband seeing her pass. He had shown practically no interest in the birth of his first child, she reasoned, so why should she show any interest in keeping him informed?

She had reached this decision after hearing Vallero tell one of his cronies that he had no intentions of attending the birth of the baby, because, as he put it, "The designer of a new boat need not be there to see the launching. I laid the keel, which completes my part of the enterprise. Basta!"

This was her baby, and by God, she'd bring the child into the world by herself.

As she approached the admissions counter at St. Mary's Hospital, however, a wrenching pain accompanied by a torrent of water down her leg caused Maria to amend her resolution slightly. "Please send someone to tell my mother that I have come," she whispered to the nurse who had seen her onset of labor and quickly helped her into a wheelchair.

Through the night, the labor pains continued at ever closer intervals as Maria fought her body to bring her child into the world. Giovanna tried to help – holding a hand that often pushed her away, applying cold cloths to a forehead that shook them off – but knew how little she could do to help her daughter's suffering. Thank the good Lord in heaven above, she said to herself, for removing all memory of this pain after it is over. If He were unable to do this, the earth would very soon become depopulated, since no woman in her right mind would want a second child.

Then as the moment of truth approached, with Dr. Scalia urging his patient to bear down just when the labor pain reached its zenith, Maria opened her eyes in a look of sheer terror and called out to anyone who could hear her: "No, no, no. I don't want to loose it."

"But you must, my child," said Giovanna firmly. "Your baby wants to be born."

Maria pressed, and then implored anyone within earshot: "Catch it. Can anyone catch it? Don't let it fall!" The baby arrived, as Giovanna laughed through her tears of joy. And Maria lay back on her pillows, exhausted, with just barely enough energy left to follow the physicians instructions and extrude the afterbirth.

At the cafe, Antonio Vallero was celebrating somewhat prematurely the birth of a child he was convinced would be a boy. While toasting the health of his son, a messenger burst through the door to announce, "You are now the father of a beautiful little baby girl."

"Girl, did you say? Huh, A girl?"

"Yes, and both mother and daughter are well, though the labor was long and difficult for your wife, Signor Vallero."

"A girl," muttered the new father as he slumped into a chair.

Meanwhile, in her sun-drenched room, Maria turned to receive her swaddled infant daughter from the hands of a nurse who had just finished cleaning her. The new mother smiled at her baby in a tableau the utter beauty of which can only be appreciated, though never described, by first hand witnesses.

Maria whispered into the baby's ear. "Rosa," kissed her shiny red face and they went to sleep. As one.

❖❖❖

News of the blessed event had already reached
the regulars of the Via Media cafe by the time the new
father arrived wearing a sheepish smile.

"Ciao, Papa Antonio. Congratulations!"

"We knew you could do it, Antonio."

"So you didn't get one with a handle, you can always
try again ..."

"And again and again and again"

"Yes, Antonio, you're always trying – very trying."

Signor Vallero was torn by mixed feelings as he let his
forced smile move from face to face of the cafe's reception committee, whose self-appointed members moved
up to shake his hand and throw their arms about his
drooped shoulders.

He felt pride in being a father and the center of attention at the place where he spent nearly all of his time
when he wasn't entering transactions into the books of
Vallero and Sons Home Furnishings store at the bottom
of the hill.

But the tone of some of his friends' salutations made
him feel uneasy. Were these friends mocking him?
Coming straight from his wife's hospital bed, where he
had been moved by a new radiance that surrounded her
and their infant, Antonio resented the way the event was
being made the object of jest bordering on ridicule. His
stomach churned.

Why did his first child have to be a girl? He knew in
his mind that this irreversible fact of life resulted form an
impartial roll of the chromosome dice. But deep down
inside, he felt that the outcome had somehow been determined by his wife, her doting mother and all of those
aunts who tolerated him only because of his wealth. This
was their way of showing him up, of showing who had
the ultimate authority in his marriage. The edge of this
feeling was rubbed raw by the sarcasm and patronizing

laughter of his buddies.

He needed a drink.

"Fuck you, and the mules you rode in on," said Vallero, who suddenly realized that only a light-hearted response would put an end to the ridicule if that's what it was. Don't let the bastards know how much it hurt. You can't hurt a person who doesn't care. Daggers thrown into polenta pudding strike nothing and disappear unnoticed. Was it not so?

"Anyway, Antonio, it doesn't change the spots on the cards," summed up Antonio's best friend, GiorgioVaccaro, as he took a pack of soiled playing cards from behind the bar.

"Have an eye-opener on the house," said the innkeeper, who alone had felt the pain suffered by Antonio. Gino Marchetti had operated the cafe ever since his father was killed in a knife fight with a patron twenty years ago. He had of necessity, developed a callous around his nerves to buffer the terrible memory of his father's death. This same protective screen enabled him to ignore the demeaning slurs that those who pay money to another feel they are entitled to make at the recipients expense. At the same time, although he would never admit it, Gino was usually aware of the hurt felt by those who hurt him.

Antonio Vallero thanked the innkeeper with a genuine smile as he tossed off the double shot of grappa (spirits distilled from the marc of pressed wine grapes) that Gino had poured into a water glass from an unlabeled bottle of the 100 proof home brew kept under the bar for special occasions.

"Come on, boys, let's deal 'em," said Giorgio, leading the way to a card table set up in the back of the room. The others followed him, unaware of any particular meaning behind Gino's free drink to Antonio. A gesture, they would say, by a person who always acted as a sort of neutral peacemaker, a Swiss businessman promoting peace and harmony in the interest of making money.

As the afternoon wore on, Antonio became increasingly disenchanted with the cronies he was playing cards with and, worse, losing money to. He was also disgusted with the source of this money: a family business that hid him away in a backroom with a quill pen, a bottle of ink and an accounts ledger while his brother represented the firm in dealings with its relatively affluent clientele, making large sales commissions that had paid for a seaside villa, a stable of thoroughbred horses and an entourage of beautiful women.

Now, the birth of a daughter had clouded the one aspect of his life that Antonio prized: his marriage to the beautiful Maria. Not only was he denied a son and heir but he knew that his wife's family, especially her mother and aunts, would make matters worse by using the bambina's presence as an excuse for imposing their own presence in his home at all hours of the night and day. Antonio had had a small foretaste of this in-law suffocation during Maria's pregnancy. The larger and sexually less accessible Maria became, the longer and more frequent became the visits of these women. Why in God's name didn't they spend more time in the fields earning money, which they could use to buy some new maternity clothes for Maria and pretty things for the baby whose appearance they awaited with the anticipation generally reserved for the hatching of heirs to the throne?

It was to escape the chattering presence of these females that Antonio had started spending more and more time at the cafe with the men whom he now realized were for the most part mere acquaintances whose primary interest in him – like that of his wife's family – was financial. So here he was, drinking too much, spending less time than ever on the job, serving as the butt of rude commentary by his wife's family and now his health was suffering. He needed some sour dark-brown hangover medicine to get his hands to stop shaking in the morning. But this produced a giddy feeling that could only be overcome with a shot of grappa with a beer chaser in the afternoon.

After the others had left for home, Antonio motioned to his best friend to join him at the bar for a drink. Just one little one, he signaled with his fingers.

"Giorgio, can I speak quite openly with you?"

"Yes, of course, Antonio, my friend. I know you've been unhappy lately. Tell me, what is wrong?"

"It's not one thing. It's a million little things. It's my job, my family, my health, these assholes that take our money at cards."

"I know. It's galling. They're lousy card players, but we can't bring ourselves to win because if we did, they'd be out of here like that," and Giorgio snapped his fingers.

"And we'd never see them again. Would that be so bad?" Antonio did not expect an answer; the question was rhetorical. Both he and Giorgio, a plumber, thought it better to be big fish in a small pond, than small fish in a larger pond. The Via Media, with its unswept floors, smoke tar-stained mirrors and the persistent odor of old cigar butts left to soak in brass spittoons that had been emptied but never cleaned, created just the right atmosphere. It made them feel superior. Large fish.

"What's the answer?" asked the pipe craftsman who had a dozen people waiting for his services, but who had for several years responded promptly only to calls from people with problems demanding emergency attention. All others could wait a few weeks, or months.

"Let's get the hell out of here," said Antonio through yellowed teeth.

"Well, you can say that. You've got money to move, a beautiful young wife and only one kid. I've got seven kids, an ugly old battleaxe and no money at all except for a few thousand lire in a tin can I've buried in the garden that she doesn't know anything about." That he would even mention his hidden savings to another person was a measure of Giorgio's trust in Antonio or his intake of grappa or a combination of both.

Antonio responded to his friend's expression of trust by slowly withdrawing from his inside jacket pocket a thick sheet of stationery that had obviously been folded and unfolded a dozen times. Leveling his buddy with a deadly serious if slightly unfocused gaze, he opened the letter, and gently rapped the paper with the back of his hand. "America," he whispered in a confidential tone, as a broad smile spread out across his face.

"What? You said 'merica'?" Giorgio's lantern jaw dropped over his throat and remained there.

"I said America and I mean America." He pronounced each syllable for emphasis. "More exactly, a small town in the state of Illinois, where my cousin wrote this letter and thousands of brothers and sisters from the Piedmont have found jobs, mostly working in mines, making good money. Like our cousins here at this very watering holes, these emigrants love to play cards, but lack the smarts to win at cards. Do you follow me?"

"Yes, I do. They are the sheep waiting to be ..."

"Sheared. I believe that's the word you're looking for, my dear friend."

"Tell you what, my dear Antonio. if I were in your boots, I'd be on a boat before the end of summer. But I can't join you, sorry to say."

"Why not?" Antonio felt his courage slipping away as he realized that he might have to make the voyage to the New World on his own. "Why can't you join me? We'll make a fortune. We ..."

"No, Antonio. Hold it. My family obligations tie me to this rude landscape like the leather straps that hold packs to the back of the mule."

"That's just the point," interjected Antonio as a ray of renewed hope lit up his face. "Here you are little more than a mule carrying packs of obligations to the grave. In America, you'll be your own man. You'll make enough money to come home and buy your own mules, as many mules as you'll ever need or want."

Shaking his head slowly, Giorgio raised up his huge body from his chair and brought forward his calloused hands, turning them slowly to reveal the scars and permanent bruises that honored a lifetime of manual labor. "These hands are made for honest labor, Antonio." One hand went up to stop the protest forming on Antonio's lips. "I know what you're about to say. And you're right. These hands have also seen their share of cards and dice and they have held in their grasp more than a few glasses of wine. And yes," Giorgio regarded his hands as if for the first time and said: "Yes, my friend, these ugly mitts will be with me all the way to my grave. Right here in the rocky soil of Valperga."

There was nothing left to say. The old friends embraced, and Giorgio left with a sad wave to the innkeeper. Antonio signalled for a double, which put him over the edge.

Maria had just finished washing up the dinner dishes when her husband made his grand entrance. After throwing open the front door with bravado befitting a man of substance, Antonio Vallero felt his dignity dissolve as he tripped on the raised threshold and plunged headlong into the dining room table, which collapsed under his considerable weight.

"Well," said Maria as she calmly folded the dish towel and hung it up. "I can only say how happy we should be that you are in a position to obtain quality furniture at wholesale prices." And against her better judgement, for she knew how vain and thin-skinned her husband could be, she laughed. It started as a chuckle half-suppressed by her hand, and would have ended there, except, as Antonio tried to brush himself off while holding onto the back of a chair for support, the chair collapsed, and he was back on the floor, legs kicking in all directions in the fashion of a frightened crab, profanity streaming from his mouth in disjointed oaths.

Maria was unable to contain herself and laughed aloud for the first time in their marriage.

"Go ahead and laugh, you miserable slut! Laugh your fat butt off instead of preparing dinner for me, as any self-respecting woman would do for her husband."

Curiously, Maria was neither angry nor frightened by his outburst, but possessed by a devilish impulse to get even for all of the times her husband had returned home in a drunken state and insisted that she serve him, first at the table and afterwards in the bedroom. "Make your own meal, you drunken sot. I ate dinner at the proper time, two hours ago," and then she had to add, "with my mother, who was kind enough to keep me company in your absence."

Too angry to hit his wife, which he knew was called for, Antonio decided to administer a worse punishment for her insolence.

"Never mind, then, you need not soil your dainty little hands preparing dinner for your husband." After pausing for effect, Antonio continued, "Now or ever again."

"What do you mean?" asked Maria as she felt her self-confidence start to drain away.

"I mean, simply this: I will no longer stand for your rude behavior and the still ruder behavior of your beloved mama and her gossiping, low-life sisters."

"And what do you plan to do, pray tell?"

"I am leaving this dung heap and all of its residents." Antonio smiled calmly.

Maria raised an eyebrow to register mild surprise for

the benefit of her husband, and said "Oh?" to provide verbal concealment for the anger that raced through her innards like a brush fire in a windstorm. Her baby daughter a dung heap resident?

"Then go," said Maria in a steady voice that belied her inner turmoil. The remark had the unintended but nonetheless killing effect of sweeping aside the platform which Antonio had constructed to deliver what he assumed would be his devastating announcement. So when he said the words, they came out hollow, empty of hurtful impact. But he said the words anyway:

"I'm leaving for America."

"Bon voyage!" said Maria, smiling.

Maria felt proud of how she had handled this unworthy husband, preserving her dignity by keeping her anger hidden from view, while his stuffy bourgeois pretensions had slid down to his ankles. Best of all, she had now transformed what might have been an idle threat into an ironclad commitment. She was rid of the lout. She went into the nursery to tell her sleeping infant the good news.

CHAPTER 3

Luigi Suardi had trouble sleeping. He could get to sleep. That was never the problem. By the time he reached his bed it was four o'clock in the morning, and he was tired of playing his accordion and singing to the heedless patrons at *The Ministry*, a noveau riche night spot in the heart of the business district in Torino. A half glass of Barbera polished off the last of the adrenaline that always flowed from contact with an audience eased the transition into unconsciousness, and at least temporarily obliterated her presence.

Ever since that performance in Valperga, Luigi had been unable to clear his mind of the unsettling picture of the young bide who had danced to his music. More than a fleeting recollection, Maria appeared to him in a way he had never before experienced and, therefore, was unable to erase. She had intruded into the very core of his being. her soft, raven locks flew about as she danced, and gave herself over, almost recklessly, to the celebration of life. And every time he came close to displacing her presence by consciously writing off her image as a ridiculous, unwarranted and unreal infatuation, she came into sharp focus, turned her sparkling, almond eyes on him and smiled. It was, and he realized with certainty would forever be, their moment.

Those deep-set eyes penetrated his consciousness with a guileless beam of hope that shone through the dark clouds of her marriage.

Every night brought the same struggle, at once exhilarating and debilitating. Try as he might, Luigi failed to get back to sleep. The effort itself added to his exhaustion and he finally resolved to see her again. Perhaps in this way, the disruptive dream would vanish. Surely, the presence of the real woman, a woman now married and a housewife, would cause her imagined presence to evaporate. Or else, could it be that ... "No," Luigi announced in a loud voice to remove the thought that the young woman shared his feelings and wanted him as much as he needed her.

"I love you," he told his pillow and fell asleep.

The driver pulled on the reins and the donkeys brought the brightly-painted carriage to a halt in the center of Valperga. Luigi remained in his seat until his innards stopped bouncing and an old woman leading a noisy young goat and two noisy young children got off. "You gonna get off here," asked the grizzled driver as he took a skirt of red wine from the *bota* that hung suspended from the roof above his seat by a frayed red woolen cord.

"Yes, yes I am," said Luigi as he slowly rose from his wicker seat and dusted the residue of dust accumulated during the four-hour ride from his black suit and the accordion case, his constant travelling companion.

Luigi had been unable to decide on how to proceed.

The closer he approached his destination the more confused he became, as he wrestled with a dozen different plans of action. He had never been shy with women, had always been able to approach them for whatever reason in a way that was inoffensive to them. He never employed any form of physical contact to make the acquaintance of a strange woman. As a rule, he rejected even the low-key "dead hand," favored by many of his comrades. This tactic involved a gentle, seemingly accidental, touch with the back of the hand to the thigh in a crowded situation, usually on a bus or railway coach.

On this particular sunny day, Luigi was physically repelled from even reviewing in his mind the techniques he had used in the past to gain access to other women. Those experiences were from an earlier life that seemed unconnected to the somehow cleaner life that had brought him to this dusty village in the Piedmont with predestined force. To regain a sense of reality and a measure of courage – after all his dream as a married woman – Luigi made for the nearest cafe, the Via Media.

"Good morning," said Luigi in the most nonchalant manner he could affect.

"A good morning to you, sir," responded Gino Marchetti, who always felt elated by the appearance of a new customer, even those who, like Luigi, bore the signs of being in transit, and would never become a regular in his place. "And how may I be of service?"

The regulars, who had just arrived from their jobs as day laborers on the permanent project of renovating the town hall, looked up from the table and turned towards the bar. Briscalla, one of the dozen or so card games that helped pass the time for them, could wait. The arrival of a stranger in town was a noteworthy occurrence in itself, and this one looked like he just might be a potential source of fresh money in the game. The house rules that had been adopted by the quartet over the years ensured that no one from outside the confines of the Via Media could ever profit from sitting in at their table.

"A draft beer would taste mighty good right about now," said Luigi, smacking his parched lips together to indicate a dusty palate.

"Long trip?" asked Gino as he began to fill a half-liter glass from the single tap.

"Yes, a couple of hours that seemed like a dozen in that rattletrap that passes for a bus."

"Yes, I know, and those roads around here, they've been working on them for two years and they're in worse shape than ever!"

"Especially that goat path from the south," interjected Giorgio, as he stood up from the card table. "You come here from Torino, perhaps?"

"Why, yes, I did," responded Luigi who was hesitant to talk about himself, but at the same time wanted to establish rapport with Maria's neighbors and be able to elicit information from them, particularly as to where he might find her.

"I am Giorgio Vaccaro," said the more communicative of the players as he thrust his hand out to shake Luigi's. "And I can tell you a little story about that rotten Torino road."

Luigi disengaged his hand from Vaccaro's iron grip and hoped that his smile would erase the brief look of pain it had produced. He quickly reached for his glass of beer, saluted the innkeeper, and took a large swallow followed by a sigh of satisfaction. But Giorgio was not to be put off.

"You see, this paisan was riding along with a friend in a wagon the other day, when he noted that there seemed to be a rabbit in a pothole in the road. 'Look, you can see the ears of that rabbit in the pothole up ahead,' he said. To which his companion replied: 'Hell, no, my man, that's no rabbit in the pothole. That's a donkey!'"

Luigi laughed politely, which set off loud laughter from the players at the card table.

"I can see you're a musician," said Gino patting the accordion case on the bar stool.

"Well, yes, I am, as a matter of fact."

"First time in Valperga?" asked Giorgio, throwing out a line to fish for an explanation of the stranger's presence.

"Well, no. As a matter of fact I was here about a year ago to provide entertainment for a wedding reception."

"Yes, of course, now I remember you. It was the wedding of our friend, Antonio ..."

"Yes, and Maria Roscio," said Gino quickly in an effort to retain control of the conversation from Georgio, who seemed to be irritating the new customer.

Happy to hear Maria's name and to be at least momentarily saved from Giorgio's attention, Luigi swung back to Gino, emptied his glass and shoved it across the bar to be refilled.

Feigning interest in the filling of his glass, Luigi then asked in a voice that he made sound as casual as possible, "It was a fine reception. The couple is still living here in Valperga I suppose?"

"Well, no. Actually the husband has gone to America?"

"America? They've gone to America, you say?" asked Luigi, scarcely able to hide his disappointment.

"Well, not exactly," said Gino, relishing this opportunity to reinforce his claim to being the best informed source of information on everything and everyone in Valperga. He paused to sharpen the stranger's curiosity before leaning over the bar and in a half whisper continued his narrative: "You see, our friend, Antonio has gone to America to seek his fortune in, uh, Illinois"

"And his young bride?" asked Luigi, his heart thumping so loud and hard that he feared the secret of his love would be revealed by its sound.

"Oh, she has remained here for the time being with her infant daughter, living with her mother. Just a ways up the street from here," he said in the casual tone of a man who knows everything, as he waved his thumb in the direction of the Roscio home.

"Well, that's too bad," mumbled Luigi. "I hope they'll get back together soon," he lied. He then tried to hide his apparent happiness behind a large swig of beer that got caught halfway down his throat and erupted in a searing cascade from his nose and mouth. "Whew, sorry," he sputtered. So, she had a child, he mused.

Regaining his composure, Luigi left a coin on the bar and took his leave. As he reached the door, Luigi turned around, bowed and bid the occupants of the cafe farewell: "Gentlemen, it was an honor and a pleasure to make your acquaintance. I hope to see you again."

"Ciao," replied the cardplayers in unison.

"Arrivederci" called the bartender as he picked up the gratuity with a knowing smile.

There was no doubt which house she lived in. The clean plaster walls and the sparkling window panes that reflected neatly tended beds of flowers bordering the path to the doorway told him that she lived here even before he spotted the small brass *Roscio* nameplate on the door. Luigi could feel the rush of blood through his veins. The thrill was strangely terrible. What should he do? He quickened his pace. What would he say if he went to the door and Maria's mother answered his knock. Which she probably would, it being her residence. As he continued along the road, pondering this next move, Luigi heard her voice. The beautiful sound of her singing a song for her baby. Her voice was clear, full of life and love. Luigi stopped to listen.

"Here my darling daughter," called Maria as she lifted her baby from her cradle, which was being rocked by

Giovanna, her grandmother.

"Don't lift her so high, Maria. It will frighten her." Maria's mama must be a beautiful woman, too, thought Luigi as he cautiously made his way up a narrow alley between two identical houses.

"Mama, you're always three months behind Rosa's development. Why, she's six weeks old now, and her legs are as strong as a full grown horse. "But not as long, I hope," said Giovanna as she bent over to kiss her grand-daughter's forehead. At that very moment Maria felt someone looking at her and turned to look over the wall that separated the backyard from a dirt road beyond which stretched a hillside covered with grapevines. It was he, it was the one man who made her feel so warm, so wanted, so important. It was the musician who understood her, who loved her in a way her husband never would.

The two lovers who had never touched one another stood transfixed sharing the thrill of acknowledging their love in deep silence.

"Maria, what is it? You look so strange," said her mother anxiously.

Maria failed to answer because she was too filled with the image of Luigi to hear her mother's voice. Giovanna walked to her daughter's side, took the baby from her and followed her gaze to Luigi.

Upon seeing the old woman, who was indeed nearly as lovely as her daughter, Luigi knew there was nothing he could do but run away. After a few faltering steps, however, he pulled himself up to look back on Maria. Feeling her firm gaze on him Luigi slowly reached into his vest pocket to remove the ancient bronze coin his father had given him on his thirteenth birthday. The image of the Emperor Hadrian was struck on it, and Luigi believed what his father had told him: that the coin would always bring good fortune to its owner, so long as he kept it shining brightly. Luigi brought the coin to his lips, turned to meet Maria's gaze, kissed the coin and carefully placed it on top of a fence post before he continued his flight.

Maria stood silently for what seemed an eternity. Suddenly she kicked open the gate in the garden wall, cried out for the man to stop, and ran as fast as she could across the field. She had no chance of catching up to Luigi, but she did get to the fence post in time to retrieve his gift to her before a group of street urchins could get to it. Maria kissed the face of the Roman emperor, slipped the coin into her blouse and returned slowly to her mother with tears clouding her eyes. Giovanna returned the baby Rosa to her cradle, then embraced her daughter and nodded slowly in understanding. Maria had no need to explain.

"I must find him, Mama. I must be with him or I'll die, because life without him is empty. It is death."

"No, my baby. I know you and I know love when I see it in the eyes of a man and a woman. You are truly in love, and one day you will be together. But not yet. you are still the wife of Antonio Vallero, married in the sight of God in His Church. You must obey the vows of the holy sacrament of marriage, my beloved daughter. your duty is clear: you must join your wedded husband."

"But Mama mia ..."

"I will help you pack."

Rosa had started to cry, big wet tears, and Maria know that her mother was right. She carried her little daughter into the bedroom and spoke to her in hushed tones about how wonderful life was going to be in the New World. Everything big and shiny. Lots of children to play with. By the time she put Rosa to bed, Maria had nearly convinced herself of a happy life awaiting in America. But her joy was overshadowed by her loss. "Please God," she prayed with her eyes burning into the wooden Crucifix above her bed, "let me be with this accordion player, or at least let him stay in my life, somewhere, somehow." And she fell asleep, with the Emperor Hadrian held tightly to her breast.

CHAPTER 4

Conditions in Steerage Class aboard the SS
Colombo bound from Genoa to New York were quite different from what Maria had imagined they would be
during the several weeks she spent preparing for the
voyage. Old relatives who had made the crossing in sailing ships and returned to die in their Piedmont homes,
painted a glossy picture that left out all the sordid details
lest Maria and, more particularly, her three-year-old
daughter became discouraged and reluctant to make the
trip. In fact, they never mentioned the crossing, but only
how wonderful everything was in the New World. What
purpose would it serve, they reasoned, to tell Maria
about hardships of an ocean voyage that she had to
endure in any case to get to where duty beckoned?

The Mediterranean, "Our Sea," as the Romans had
proudly named it in ancient times, was kindly enough.
Its deep blue waters that shimmered in bright sunlight
during the day and glowed in the light of a full moon at

night seemed to caress the ship. The air was sweet up on deck where Maria kept Rosa most of the time to escape the darkness and the sweaty bulkheads of their assigned space on D deck, four decks below the main deck and two decks below the water line.

The North Atlantic was different. An hour west of the Straits of Gibraltar, the ship began to roll from side to side and pitch up and down in a way that suggested the vessel had suddenly lost control of its senses. An able-bodied seaman old enough to have served on squarerig-gers observed Maria slipping on the deck and helped her to a rope attached to a hold covering in the middle of the ship where both rolling and pitching were felt less than at other locations.

"Thank you, sir, for your help," Maria told her bene-factor. "I'm beginning to feel so light-headed, almost dizzy," she added. Is this what they call mal de mer?"

"Well, ma'm, the old sea affects different people in different ways. Some in the head, others in the stomach. You're one who suffers in the head, and a very pretty one, too, if I may say so."

Maria acknowledged the tribute with a smile that briefly illumined that part of her face that appeared under the bright red bandanna her mother had given her as a farewell present. It had been filled with cakes, long since eaten. "But what should I do about it. I feel so giddy."

"Tell you what," said the old salt, "what you want to do is what you shouldn't do."

"And what's that?" asked Maria through a forced half smile.

"Wouldn't it be pleasant to lie down and just let the motion of the sea rock you and your little girl to sleep?"

"Oh, yes, I think it would" said Maria as she put her infant on her hip and moved towards the ladder leading to the deck below.

"No," said the sailor as he gently forced mother and daughter to resume their positions atop the hold cover. "Like I said, that would be the worst thing you could do. You'll feel so comfortable lying down that you'll not want to get up. Then, either you'll have to stay lyin' down all the way across, or it'll hit you in the stomach, and you'll have to run up on deck to heave your guts overboard, if you'll pardon the expression."

"Then what should we do?"

"Stay right here and breathe the fresh salt air. Breathe in when the bow of the ship goes up and breathe out when she comes back down. And pretty soon you'll feel like you're right at home on the old Atlantic, just like the fella from Genoa who gave his name to this here ship: Cristobal Colon Columbo. Rest his soul."

"We'll try. And thank you!" Maria shouted after the sailor.

It was at the apex of one of her deeper inhalations that Maria saw him, standing at the railing just forward and above where she sat. Or was it he? She couldn't be sure because of the ocean spray that distorted her vision. When she had wiped her eyes clear and looked up again, the man had turned as another person led him through an open doorway into the Cabin Class lounge. Could it be my musician? Is he here performing for the passengers in the higher classes on the higher decks?

She was right on both counts. Luigi had heard from Gino, whose cafe he came to visit every day he was free from his job, about Maria's impending departure for America to rejoin her husband. Driven by his desire to be near her, Luigi had been able to get free passage on the Colombo as payment for his musical services. As much as he wanted to go to her, Luigi knew he had no right. Furthermore, there would be time to see her, be with her, on the other side of the Atlantic. He was somehow sure of it.

It was getting late and Maria had to go below with Rosa, who had been running a fever for several days. No sooner had they gotten nestled into their allotted wooden bunk space than an elderly passenger a short distance away threw up. Fortunately someone had handed him a large soup bowl to prevent the vomit from falling on the deck, unfortunately, he had tripped over the leg of a fellow passenger and spilled the bowl's contents, which splattered over a large area of huddled humanity. Amid curses and cries, the unfortunate passenger escaped up the single ladder that provided access to the open deck.

Maria looked the other way and covered her daughter's eyes and ears in her shawl. The incident had seemingly passed when a little mutt of a dog sauntered over to the vomit and began to eat it. Eight days had gone by and there were another four or five days to go before the Colombo would arrive in New York. Maria ran up two decks with her daughter in her arms, swept aside a protesting shipping lines sentry dressed in black at the top of the second ladder to a door marked with a large red cross, where she stopped to catch her breath before knocking on the dispensary door. A nurse opened the door and tried to keep Maria out to no avail.

"I must see a doctor, my daughter is sick," she said in a firm voice that concealed her desperation, and she moved past the nurse into the presence of Doctor Riccardi.

Maria looked up at the tall man in a white coat. She knew at once that he was her guardian angel, sent in answer to the prayers she whispered almost continuously over the fevered brow of her infant daughter, whose illness had made them both too weak to cry. "My little baby is so sick, Doctor," moaned the distraught mother in a voice choked by anxiety. In supplication, she kept her glistening dark eyes on the angular face of the middle-aged physician, who loomed at least a foot above her.

Doctor Riccardi recognized the look. He had seen it cloud the face of his mother-in-law as she informed him of the street accident which caused the death of his wife and two-year-old son less than a year ago.

"Let me see her, dear child," said Dr. Riccardi as he bent down and with a movement both gentle and strong, took the bundled baby from Maria and sensed the trembling in the mother's breast as he did so. Quickly reassured by his deep voice and confident manner, Maria released her child to him after a brief moment of instinctive hesitation. "Yes, she is, as you say," Maria hesitated and looked at her benefactor with a quizzical smile, "a dear child."

"But I was referring to ..." Dr. Riccardi stopped, his train of thought derailed as he contemplated this strangely vulnerable yet strong young woman.

"To me, Doctor?"

"To you, my dear child."

Doctor Riccardi wondered why he said that as he tried to unravel the tangled emotions produced by this troubled Steerage Class waif who had barged into his dispensary unannounced. How could it be that in a few moments she had managed to pierce through his professional armor and straight into the very depths of his being.

Guido Riccardi, Doctor of Medicine, refused the helping hand of his nurse, who customarily performed the preliminary work of taking the temperature of patients and making them ready for his examination. "You may take off the rest of the day, Sister Lucia," he had said, adding "You've been a great help on this busy day and deserve some rest."

After first checking for symptoms of life-threatening disease, especially dreaded diphtheria and meningitis, the doctor expertly swaddled the infant and gently placed her in a bassinet in a darkened corner of the cabin.

As he turned to talk with the sick child's mother, whom
he assumed would be in the waiting room, he bumped
into her. "Oh, excuse me, my, uh, Senora. I am pleased to
tell you that your beautiful little girl will be all right."

"Oh, thank God," whispered Maria as she collapsed
into the arms of Dr. Riccardo.

When she awoke several hours later, Maria looked up
to see the doctor standing over her, looking into her eyes,
smiling. He was taking her pulse an she dared not speak
until he took his hand from her wrist. She felt warmed by
his presence and returned his smile. "How is my baby?"
she asked in a surprisingly strong voice.

"She is much better already, Senora. She has a rather
nasty case of dysentery, which is quite common in steer
..., that is, on board ship.

"Is it serious? Where is she? How long will ...?"

"Please, one question at a time. You are also stricken
with the same malady. You, like your little girl need lots
of fluids and rest, plenty of rest You can get both right
here in my little hospital. To make room for the two of
you, I just released a grand dame from Austria, who was
unnecessarily occupying a bed with a mild case of sea
sickness compounded by a severe case of loathing for her
fifth husband. She wanted to stay here for the entire
crossing.

"I can't say that I blame her," said Maria impishly,
and paused before explaining: "I don't know how this
accommodation compares with the old lady's cabin in
First Class, but I can tell you that it is a large step above
Steerage Class."

"Yes, I know it is. Conditions in that area are worse
than sub-standard, they're sub-human. Something must
be done to prevent the shipping lines from leasing that
space below deck to entrepreneurs whose sole interest is
to make as much money as possible. Naturally, this
means that they'll sell as many tickets as possible, with-

out a second thought as to what ill effects the over-
crowding will have on the health and safety of all those
poor passengers.

"What's worse," the good doctor continued, "I'm not
even allowed to provide medical assistance to passengers in Steerage Class. And about a tenth of them died on
our last two crossings. Why, according to regulations, I
should deny treatment to you and your little girl."

"Thank you, Doctor, for breaking the rules and coming to our assistance," said Maria as she took her savior's
hand turned its palm to her lips and kissed it softly,
unhurriedly.

My God, thought Riccardi. Have you sent this most
beautiful woman to me to ease my suffering? Are she
and her lovely child meant to replace the wife and child
who were so cruelly taken from me? Yes, this must be the
mysterious way You have acted so that I shall be able to
overcome my disabling loss. And be able to minister to
the medical needs of your children during the rest of my
days. "Oh, merciful God, I thank you," whispered the
man who until this moment had considered himself an
agnostic.

As if attuned to the new happiness of this unlikely
couple, the weather backed off with a smile, The sea
replaced its churning crests and kettles with long curv-
ing swells that seemed to embrace the ship and move it
forward to its glorious destination: the city of New York
in the United States of America. Maria and Rosa, having
recovered from their illness, stayed in the dispensary for
the rest of the voyage. Dr. Riccardi said they had to
remain there to prevent the spread of their disease to
their fellow passengers and Maria put up only a token
show of opposition to the doctor's orders, which she
knew were more out of affection for her than for any
great concern with the health of her compatriots in
Steerage. Unlike the hell of life below the water line, the

days on Promenade Deck were pure bliss. The difficulty of communicating verbally, because of the chasm between the Italian dialects spoken in Maria's Piedmont and Guido's Rome, was effectively bridged by the universal language of love supplemented when needed by the use of English, a language which the doctor handled with a high degree of fluency and which Maria struggled to master as his pupil on deck by day and in his cabin in the evenings. Even Rosa was taught to utter a few sounds resembling the language that would soon become her mother tongue.

One morning after a long night of half-speed progress through a pea-soup flog the S.S. Colombo entered the shipping lane into New York harbor and there she stood, illuminated by the warm rays of the morning sun. The Statue of Liberty caused the ship to list visibly a a result of so many passengers moving to the port side straining their eyes for a glimpse of her. Awakened by the deep-throated groan of the ship's horn, Maria and Riccardi moved out on deck in the semi-secluded upper deck area outside the dispensary. "She's so majestic," whispered Maria, fearful that a raised voice would break the spell. "Indeed," said Riccardi, as he enfolded his beloved in his arms to stifle her shivering in the damp morning air. Maria nestled into his warming embrace like a kitten in the arms of a sleeping child. Both closed their eyes, the better to suck out of this moment every drop of ecstatic pleasure and make it last forever. All the world was at peace. *E per un mument tut el mund lera tranquil.*

After half an hour that lasted all day, the cacophony of whistles, horns, throbbing tugboat engines and guttural shouts from the stevedores working pier 42 on the Hudson River broke through their seemingly invincible serenity and plunged doctor and patient into the harsh reality of the dirtiest, noisiest, most crime-ridden and exciting port in the world. In only a few minutes they would separate, with little hope of ever meeting again. On the previous evening, Dr. Riccardi tried to persuade Maria to remain aboard ship for at least the week that the vessel usually remained in port. He had nearly convinced her with the argument that there might still be traces of the disease that had infected her and Rose, and if the medical examiners of the Immigration Service discovered this, they might be denied entry into the New World or at best be detained in unsavory conditions at the Ellis Island holding pen for days or even weeks.

Maria considered the doctor's advice on rational grounds for several minutes before letting her intuitive feelings decide the matter: if she remained on the ship, she would never be able to bring herself to leave Guido Riccardi. While this alternative offered an undeniably pleasing prospect, it would represent a betrayal of her mother's wishes as well as her sacred marriage vows. Maria knew she must leave, and did so, without looking back to the man who, in a final act of love, had seen to it that she and her daughter would be able to get onto the first ferry boat departing from the side of the S.S. Colombo for Ellis Island.

Like all of the First and Second Class passengers, Luigi Suardi had received his immigration papers after a brief examination by Immigration officers in the Lounge and crossed the gangplank onto the pier, bypassing Ellis Island.

CHAPTER 5

"Give me your tired, your poor, your huddled masses yearning to breathe free ..." The greeting inscribed on the Statue of Liberty burned a personal message into Maria's consciousness, and she memorized it. When the ferry boat tied up at the entrance to Ellis Island, she repeated the words over and over in an effort to subdue the anxiety that enveloped her hope as she beheld the imposing French Renaissance-style building that served as the gateway to a new and hoped for better life in the New World for millions of immigrants. It was a grand structure, much finer than the old wooden building, described by the then Immigration Commissioner Joseph Senner as "a row of unsightly, ramshackle tinderboxes" that mercifully had burned to the ground in 1897. But somehow, its very bulk and the studied symmetry of the new building's design suggested a place where inhumanity was institutionalized, a cold place.

The emigrants from her home town who had returned from the U.S. had warned Maria of several dangers that she should expect to encounter in New York. First of all, she should be wary of corrupt officials at the immigration facility, who would offer her all kinds of favors up to and including certificates of citizenship in exchange for monetary or other "considerations." Her youthful beauty, her advisers told Maria, could be a mixed blessing when viewed by the rude people she was apt to encounter in the immigration facility, including interpreters and officials whose uniforms, white shirts and ties, gave them a deceptively honest appearance. In the same boat were the official money changers, who exchanged foreign currencies into dollars at a quarter or less of their official value. The crooked money changers usually included in their payment for foreign currencies a large number of shiny pennies, whose gleam fooled many a newcomer into attributing to them a higher value than their actual worth.

Forewarned as she was, Maria had gotten the good doctor Riccardi to change the packet of lira she retrieved from its hiding place in the lining of her petticoat into dollars at what appeared to her to be a highly favorable rate of exchange. Without questioning the amount of dollars, she had put most of the new currency back into the hiding place in her undergarment, putting only a few coins in the black velvet purse embroidered by her mother's loving hands.

Carrying her daughter in her arm, Maria moved slowly from the gangplank onto solid land for the first time in weeks. She felt unsteady but knew that she must show no signs of weakness lest she be detained for medical reasons. So she walked with a forced light step under the glass canopy and into the reception hall, or Main Building, as it was called. There a porter coarsely but not unkindly called on the huddled masses trudging before

him to "step lively there, you cattle. You'll soon find a
nice little pen." The livestock analogy was apt, as all of
the new arrivals carried brands in the form of cardboard
manifest tags pinned to their outer garments providing
the name of the ship on which they arrive, their names
and countries of origin. When entering the main hall, the
immigrants were directed into parallel lines separated by
white-painted plumbing pipes that led to the medical
examiners, who looked like well-dressed livestock
judges at a county fair. The doctors had already made
preliminary diagnoses as they observed the immigrants
walk across an open space of some 20 feet. After a cursory examination, the lapels of some of the new arrivals
were inscribed with one or more letters of chalk: "H" for
possible heart problems, "F" for facial rash, "X" for mental retardation or the most dreaded circled "K" denoting
insanity. All immigrants, including children of all ages,
were checked for trachoma, a contagious eye disease,
which was relatively common in southern Europe at that
time. When a thumb-raised eyelid revealed traces of the
disease that could lead to blindness, the victims were
denied admission to the United States and sent back
home, often as passengers on the same liners that had
brought them to the New World. Conjunctivitis ("pink
eye") was occasionally mistakenly diagnosed as trachoma, barring the unfortunate sufferer of this common
ailment from entering the country.

Mental illness was another diagnosis made by medi-
cally-untrained inspectors to keep would-be immigrants
from ever setting foot on the mainland of America.

One of the Colombo passengers, a young maiden
from a Piedmont village not far from Maria's home, was
literally driven crazy by the intrusive investigations of a
doctor who was called on to check her out by inspectors
who were unable to understand her strange dialect, even
with the aid of an Italian-speaking interpreter. The girl

had never before been permitted to be in the company of a man without a chaperone, and suddenly here was a strange man who rapped her knees with a mallet and stroked her spinal column beneath her dress in an effort to check her reflexes. The poor girl, Maria later learned, had reacted so violently to what she took to be untoward advances by the doctor that she was judged to be insane and sent home. Maria avoided a similar fate thanks to her knowledge of basic English, which she quickly switched to whenever the interpreter failed to understand her dialect.

To speed up her processing, Maria had taken care to leave her daughter's diaper unchanged. After a cursory medical examination, the beautiful young mother and her innocently soiled, bawling daughter were moved hastily up to and through the immigration inspector's desk. With immigration permit in hand (there being no passports or green cards in those days) Maria was shown to the ladies room where she quickly changed and fed little Rosa. Out in the fresh autumn air at last, Maria inhaled deeply and whispered her thanks to God for her successful journey. Before her arrival, this place had processed millions of immigrants who enriched their adopted land with their talents: songwriter Irving Berlin, who came over from Russia in 1892; football coach Knut Rockne from Norway a year later; Samuel Goldwyn from Poland en route to Hollywood in 1896; movie director Frank Capra from Italy in 1903; actor Edward G. Robinson from Rumania in 1903; and Bob Hope from England in 1908.

From 1892, when it was built until its closing in 1954, Ellis Island ushered in the ancestors of four out of every ten Americans. In 1912, when Maria and Rosa appeared in the Port of New York, 605,151 persons representing roughly three quarters of the total number of immigrants to enter the U.S. that year passed through the storied halls.

Thanks to reforms initiated by Teddy Roosevelt and carried out for the most part by his two-term appointee, New York attorney William Williams, the corruption that plagued Ellis Island in its early years had largely been eliminated. Which is not to say that all of the vermin preying on the more or less helpless immigrants had been eradicated.

"Now, who have we here?," asked the gentleman who stood at the curbside in front of the Main Building. At least Maria supposed him to be a gentleman the way he took off his derby and held it in his hand while he made a deep bow in her direction. The grey spats, the likes of which she had never before seen, protecting the tops of his shiny black shoes confirmed her image of what a gentleman must look like. "Could it be a lovely lady from Italy and her charming daughter?" he asked in a friendly voice warmed by resonance like the voice of Luigi Suardi, the accordion player who was never far from her thoughts.

"Indeed," she responded in Italian through in impish smile. "Have you waited long?"

"A lifetime, madame, but as they say" 'he who waits for something good never waits in vain.'"

His Italian marked the stranger as an educated man of good family, probably from Milano or Torino judging from his azure blue eyes.

"They say that, do they?"

"Yes, they do. Now please allow me to offer you my services."

"Oh?" replied Maria, feigning milk shock at his bold-ness," and what kind of services do you offer us?"

"That depends on your needs, Madame. Is it possible that you require transportation?"

"Why, yes, I suppose we must leave this lovely island sooner or later," she said as she turned her head to one

side and gazed into his eyes with the suggestion of a
smile playing at the corner of her mouth.

"Then off we go," he said as he took her valise in one
hand and hoisted Rosa up onto his shoulder with the
other hand.

Strong, too, thought Maria, who was impressed by her
daughter's immediate acceptance of this strange man
without so much as a whimper.

"The ferry to Manhattan should leave in a few minutes," he said. "And there we can take my carriage to
whatever destination you choose."

"Let's go, then," said Maria, who stopped suddenly
as if she had forgotten something. She impulsively laid
her hand on the stranger's arm to get him to stop while
she took a final look back at the Main Building, smiled
and whispered, "Ciao, my friend."

On the cramped ferry, women in babushkas looked
enviously at Maria. Some people get all the breaks, their
eyes said as they admired the tall man they assumed to
be her husband. Her escort said nothing until the little
boat reached the Battery at the tip of Manhattan. He then
helped Maria onto the dock and pointed to a carriage
standing nearby. "There we are," he said, motioning to
the driver to fetch them, as if the carriage and driver
belonged to him.

A bit too smooth, thought Maria, who noticed that the
carriage driver seemed in no hurry to respond to the call
for his services.

"Where shall we go now?" asked the man, who interrupted Maria's silence by adding, "Oh, excuse me, my
name is Daniel Giardello. I live here in Manhattan."

What could he have been doing on Ellis Island, she wondered. "My name is Signora Maria Roscio Vallero. We
need to get to the railway station to get a train to Spring
Valley where I will join my husband."

"And where, might I ask is Spring Valley?" he asked

in a politely sarcastic tone.

"Why, it is in the state of Illinois," answered Maria as if anyone should know that simple piece of American geography.

As they pulled up at Central Station, the man alighted, instructed the driver in English to wait a few minutes for his return, then turned to Maria: "My dear lady, it is like a zoo inside the station, so I will go in and purchase tickets for you and your daughter and then come back to help you get to the train. When Maria hesitated, he continued: "I have instructed my driver to wait here with you while I am inside."

Maria saw from the expression on the driver's face that he had never worked for the man who claimed to be his employer.

"That's very kind of you, Sir, but I think we'll manage without your help. You've done enough for us already, and I thank you very much."

"Well at least let me help you in with your bag," he said as he paid off the driver, explaining that he was giving "his man" some money to go get himself something to eat.

Inside the bustling terminal, the stranger once again asked for money to buy her tickets, which he said would cost about fifty dollars.

"No," said Maria in a tone that left no room for discussion. "We can manage. Thank you and goodbye."

The last word was shouted so as to reach the ears of a policeman she had seen standing by a shoeshine stand about 30 feet distant. The man then grabbed Maria's purse and started to walk away, confident that the little woman would never abandon her daughter to give chase. Although the purse was devoid of anything but sentimental value, Maria saw no reason why this thief should have it, and she screamed at the top of her considerable voice: "Stop thief," first in Italian and then in

English. The policeman apprehended the man and brought him back to Maria. "Would you," he asked, "like to press charges against this man?"

"No," said Maria in English, and then said to the man in Italian: "It is a severe enough sentence that he must live with himself and behold his thieving face in the mirror every time he shaves." Whereupon she swung her returned purse in a wide semi-circle, bringing it across his face and leaving a jagged cut on the bridge of his nose.

"I repeat what I said before. 'Thank you, Sir, and goodbye.'"

Maria then turned to the policeman and with a subdued voice, like that of a helpless waif, asked if he would be kind enough to help her buy railway tickets to Spring Valley.

"As you probably know, Sir, that's in the state of Illinois."

"I'd be happy to help you, M'am," he said and carried her bag to the ticket counter. He then offered to hold her youngster while she purchased her tickets.

"Thank you," said Maria and gave the constable a warm smile of gratitude.

CHAPTER 6

Luigi Suardi had never experienced anything like
this. He was drowned with waves of mixed emotions
centered on his beautiful Maria. How her eyes sparkled
as she stood by the railing with her hands protectively
held on the shoulders of her pale daughter as the two of
them silently viewed the grand lady holding aloft a torch
that would light their future. How magically her long
tresses, blown loose by gusting harbor winds, had covered and then unveiled the smiling face that had become
indelibly imprinted on his sensory screen.

And then there was that older man wearing the uniform of a ship's officer who had provided Luigi with
pills against seasickness on the first day out, who
appeared at the side of Maria as the ship docked. They
spoke to each other in a way that ruled out a merely
casual relationship between them. And when they had
embraced, a sensible void swallowed up Luigi Suardi.

All the beauty that had filled his eye and mind was erased, leaving only questions: How could Maria embrace this man? how had they met? how long and how intimately had they known each other? had they perhaps arranged to meet on the ship and share the doctor's first class cabin during the entire crossing?

Luigi could not bear to look, yet his gaze was drawn back to them by that mysterious force that compels us to focus on repulsive objects, such as the unappetizing contents of spittoons and toilet bowls.

The embrace that had shorted out his nervous system was mercifully unprolonged, and Luigi quickly regained his senses. He could smell the salt-rotten pier pilings and the tar of the quays; hear the squeals of crane winches crying out for grease and the multilingual cursing of stevedores as they fought for the right to carry the baggage of first class passengers and kicked aside the rope-tied bags of steerage passengers. He stared at the giant buildings of Manhattan illuminated by the morning sunshine struggling to break through the sooty haze crawling up out of the smokestacks of ships and factories. Best of all, he had awakened from his sensory blackout to see that Maria never looked back as she led her daughter across the gangplank onto the Ellis Island ferry boat.

Why, the doctor might have been an old acquaintance from home, reasoned Luigi. Or maybe, though this was difficult to believe, this man may have been family, an old uncle perhaps. Hadn't the boys at the Via Media told him that the Roscios were a large family with branches that stretched from the Po River Valley all the way up to the Cottian Alps along the border of France?

It must be nice to retain close ties with family spread all over the province, thought Luigi. His own family members were concentrated in and around Turino but only rarely communicated with each other. Indeed, close-knit was a concept of family life that the Suardi's refused to share with the great majority of their countrymen. Attendance at family weddings and funerals was, of course, mandatory. So, it was one's duty to get all dressed up and put in an appearance. But desire never accompanied this duty except in the case of some of the younger female members of the extended family motivated by the remote possibility of meeting a marriageable distant cousin. Luigi had noticed that these girls, who pretended to enjoy these affairs, were dumpy little things with brightly painted lips whose miserable future lives could be seen in the heavy-lidded eyes and propped up watermelon breasts of their mothers. No, come to think of it, maybe it wouldn't be all that nice to have family close by all the time. Maybe weddings and funerals were quite enough. At least at these reunions there was always plenty of wine to produce a laugh and a good song.

In the Torino region where Luigi grew up, life was more industrialized, more modern, moved at a faster pace and was less tied to tradition and religion than in the grape and olive tree agricultural regions further to the east. Luigi wondered if he would be altogether happy trading the excitement of his way of life for the more structured and predictable life of Maria's village.

"But what the hell," shouted Luigi, as he ran down the steps of the pier and into the street where he narrowly avoided being hit by a horse-drawn baggage carriage, whose driver was more concerned with getting an eye-opener from his pocket flask of whiskey than in avoiding any impediments, be they human or in the form of concrete pillars, to the fulfillment of his assigned baggage transportation quota.

"Hey, where the hell you go?" shouted Luigi.

"Where I damn well wanna go, you foreign piece of shit," replied the teamster.

As bystanders looked on in amazement, wondering

how this lunatic got past the Immigration inspectors, Luigi slowed down and took a deep breath as he got into line to catch a streetcar for Central Station. "All I know," he said under his breath, "is that I am going to Spring Valley, Illinois, and I am one day going to meet the young woman of my dreams." And, God willing, he thought to himself, I am going to marry her. The thought warmed him, and he held onto it with all his strength until an icy blast of air carrying the first snow of the winter wrenched Luigi back to reality. He pulled his collar up against the wind and the equally frigid stares of his new compatriots and smiled at the pain and joy of being in this exciting new place. The immigrant only once glanced back down the dirty west side street that stuck steel and concrete piers like arrows into the side of the majestic Hudson River.

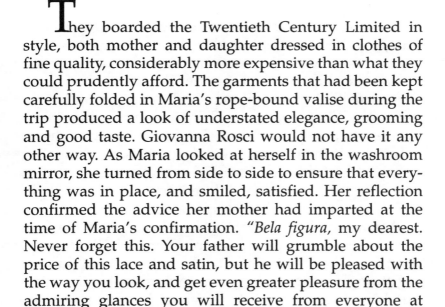

❖❖❖

They boarded the Twentieth Century Limited in style, both mother and daughter dressed in clothes of fine quality, considerably more expensive than what they could prudently afford. The garments that had been kept carefully folded in Maria's rope-bound valise during the trip produced a look of understated elegance, grooming and good taste. Giovanna Rosci would not have it any other way. As Maria looked at herself in the washroom mirror, she turned from side to side to ensure that everything was in place, and smiled, satisfied. Her reflection confirmed the advice her mother had imparted at the time of Maria's confirmation. *"Bela figura,* my dearest. Never forget this. Your father will grumble about the price of this lace and satin, but he will be pleased with the way you look, and get even greater pleasure from the admiring glances you will receive from everyone at church. believe me, you must present a respectable image at all times, my sweet child. You never know when you will be seen in public, or by whom," Giovanna Rosci had intoned, with a loving index finger waving at the ceiling to orchestrate her point. Her mother had again dipped deeply into the family savings to pay for the materials she used in sewing the figure-flattering black dress that now seemed to embrace Maria's rounded body. It was designed to serve as an all-purpose garment that would be both attractive and suitable attire for ladies whether strolling in the park or taking tea in the parlor. The dress was hidden, without concealing its contents, under a dark gray woolen coat trimmed at the neck and sleeves with sheep's wool died and curled to resemble fashionable Persian lamb. Maria's toddling daughter was dressed exactly like her mother, to the delight of their fellow passengers. Little did anyone suspect that this exquisite mother-daughter outfit was born of economic necessity rather than the creative genius of Paris dress designers.

Rosa made friends easily. Fluency in her adopted language, which she was introduced to as the only way to communicate with the youngsters of various nationalities on the ship, continued to develop in the basic conversations that unite children of all countries and backgrounds. What your name? Where you come from? Where you going? Far from being a problem, the delightful comparison of different words for the same things out the mouths of children from different countries served as social pegs for both the children and, with only slight embarrassment, their parents.

Maria wondered how she could have gotten along in conversations with her fellow passengers without Rosa. As it was, she could join in the laughter at Rosa's amusing struggles with the language to disguise her own limited knowledge of English. Language barriers also had a way of disappearing, or at least losing their intimidation, under the avalanche of dialects that filled the air in this great American melting pot. An elderly Italian from Sicily, for example, had tried in vain for several hours to cultivate contact with Maria, until finally both parties found to their amusement that the best way to communicate was in a highly disjointed and ungrammatical brand of English. Thus, although she had been in America for only a few days, Maria felt right at home with this strange new tongue which explained with a mad logic that, in the words of the Sicilian gentleman, "a blueberry is red when it is green!"

By the time the train pulled into the Illinois Central station in Chicago, Maria felt comfortable in her new homeland. She had been in the USA for less than a week, but already she had attended Christmas Mass at the glorious St. Patrick's Cathedral on Fifth Avenue and ridden a thousand kilometers on the fastest train in the world from New York City to America's second largest city, Chicago. She got off the train and for the fourth time got out her long rail ticket to make sure that the onward journey to Joliet was still covered. Yes, everything was in order. They had three hours between trains.

After checking her baggage, Maria took Rosa's hand and led her to the exit on Michigan Avenue to stretch their legs and catch a breath of fresh air. An icy blast nearly knocked Rosa to the sidewalk, and a strange feeling suddenly enveloped Maria. She thought, no, she knew that something very strange, very evil was about to happen. She rushed Rosa back inside the station, wrapped her arms about her little daughter and closed her eyes.

Huddled there, at that moment, Maria saw a man in her mind's eye. He was somewhere nearby. A shot rang out close behind him, and the man fell to the ground. But the vision was not yet finished, as two other men appeared from behind the man and somehow fastened him to the back of the black car that dragged the victim along the street for several blocks, until the vision faded as fast as it had come.

Shaken and emotionally drained, Maria took her little girl into her arms and carried her into the shelter of the station's bustling coffee shop. Several cups of coffee helped Maria to get through her terror.

"Mama, what's the matter? Are you sad?"

"No, I'm all right, Rosa. I'm fine. I just wish I knew ..."

"Knew what, Mama?"

"Never mind, my sweet baby. It was just something I imagined."

"Imagined?"

"Yes, like something I thought I saw that I didn't really see at all. You know what I mean?

"No, Mama."

"Well, never mind, I feel fine now. And it's about time to catch our train. Won't that be fun to ride on another train?"

"Yes, Mama."

Maria had nearly succeeded in freeing her psyche from the terrible experience in Chicago when her eye was drawn to newsstand in the Joliet depot. There a bold headline leaped out at her over the photo of the man she had imagined being shot earlier in the day. It appeared on the front page of a special Extra Edition of the Chicago Tribune. The caption identified the man as Charles Moyer, President of the Miners' Union, who had been shot in the back by an unidentified gunman and dragged through the streets of Chicago. Moyer accused coal mine owners of the criminal action.

Maria was shaken by a new and powerful sense of foreboding stronger than before. Partly she feared that the shooting might be related to some misfortune that awaited her in the coal mining town of Spring Valley, but the main source of her anxiety was the realization that she was blessed – or perhaps cursed – with an inexplicable power to experience events that were outside her immediate presence.

In the case of the Moyer shooting, the event took place only a few blocks from where Maria had stood inside the railway station. Had she seen it before it happened, while it happened or after it happened? She had no idea.What she did now with certainty was that her perception of the shooting had been as real, or somehow even more real, than if she had stood beside the victim when the shot was fired.

Another strange thing happened on the train ride from Chicago to Joliet for which Maria could find no explanation. It may have been the stressful hours in the windy city or the flat farmland that stretched to the horizon in a mesmerizing monotony, or a combination of both, that caused Maria and her daughter to fall into a deep sleep within five minutes after embarking on the last leg of their long journey. Sleep had overtaken them so suddenly that Maria had neglected to take a blanket from the overhead rack to cover up against the cold that seeped through the window along with the fine-grain coal soot from the engine. Yet, when the conductor came through to announce their imminently arrival at the Joliet station, Maria awoke to discover the source of her warmth: somehow, two railroad blankets had been snugly wrapped around both herself and Rosa. Probably it was the the conductor, she thought, and rewarded the old gentleman with a big smile as he came through to announce the trains' arrival in Joliet with an unnecessary warning, "don't forget your umbrellas." A few steps beyond her seat, the conductor tucked his Hamilton pocket watch back into his vest and turned to look back at the travellers with a questioning frown that slowly melted into a broad smile. "May I help you with your bags, Madame?" Feigning surprise, Maria responded, "Oh, si, thank you, thank you very much, uh, sir."

And so it was that Maria Roscio Vallero was helped from the Illinois Central big city train to the crowded, westbound local branch of the Chicago, Ottawa and Peoria railroad, known by its passengers as the *Interurban*, and into the rambunctious small town world of Spring Valley, Illinois.

CHAPTER 7

Spring Valley was founded in 1884, on gently
rolling hills sculpted by ungentle glaciers that covered
the land before retreating northward to create and then
drown in the waters of Lake Michigan. Left behind a few
hundred feet beneath the surface of the rich soil covering
most of the state were thick veins of bituminous coal.
This fuel for the industrial revolution, which was in the
process of transforming economic and social conditions
and their political consequences throughout the world,
was what gave life and rapid early development to the
region.

There on the banks of Spring Creek sprouted a typical midwestern mining boom town, populated by one-
way ticketed immigrants from more than 30 different
national homelands, most of them coming out of the bottom end of a rigid class structure that was grudgingly
succumbing to the unrelenting assault of egalitarian
social dynamics at work in the New World, where titles

were replaced by earthy nicknames, often unflattering, always worn with pride; churches of all faiths and denominations to serve their members' bonds of love and hate, outnumbered only by saloons, those last strongholds of male domination soon to be wiped out permanently by Constitutional Amendments that granted women the right to vote and withheld from men the right to drink together in public; and, a reputation for bareknuckled toughness embodied in middleweight champion of the world Billy "The Illinois Thunderbolt" Papke. Like most kids in "The Valley," Papke had worked in the mines as a teenager. This was neither unusual nor widely criticized in a period when laws limiting the working hours for women and children were being considered for the first time and six- and seven-year-old girls often worked 13-hour shifts in textile mills. One cotton mill owner openly defended this practice as "a matter of charity," the children being better off in the mills than on the loose "learning the first lessons of a vagrant's life." In the raw competition of this dog-eat-dog world in which nice guys finished last with scant sympathy accorded them, few eyebrows were raised by the questionable manner by which the German-American fighter from Spring Valley won his world title in a bloody 12th-round knockout of the legendary Stanley Ketchel, "The Michigan Assassin." Ignoring the Marquis of Queensberry custom of touching gloves with this opponent at the start of the first round, Papke seized the opportunity offered by Ketchel's lowered gloves to deliver a fierce right to the face of the champion, who had won their first encounter. Ketchel never recovered from the sucker punch and suffered his only loss to a fighter of his own weight. By the time Maria and her daughter arrived at the depot, Spring Valley was home to 7,914 people, half of whom worked in the four mines operated by the Spring Valley Coal Company, which owned the land and much of the retail business of the city. On July 4, 1894, more than 300 miners, who were earning wages of three dollars per day, offered to work without pay if the company would provide free rent, fuel, food and clothing for their families. Company town, boom town, USA 1914.

Maria wakened with a shiver as the conductor announced the Interurban's next stop as Spring Valley. It was dark and cold, and the thought of being reunited with her husband failed to provide needed warmth. As always in situations of this kind, when despair threatened to drown her spirit, Maria touched the Rosary given to her by her mother, which had become as much a part of her as the child cuddled on her bosom. She moved her lips in prayer as she made a small Sign of the Cross: In the name of the Father, and of the Son, and of the Holy Spirit. Amen. Hail Mary, full of Grace ... The car jolted her communion and Maria wakened her child, "Here we are, my sweet Rosa. Wake up, darling. Soon we shall be in our new home." The child awoke with a smile that struck straight into her mother's innermost being, into the area reserved for her prayers, to deliver a strengthening message of unconditional love. The damp cold that had enveloped Maria only moments before disappeared.

Luigi Suardi stood in the shadow of the baggage trolley cast by the kerosene lamp swaying from the roof over the wooden planked station platform. The gusts of wintry air crept through the seams of his woolen jacket like a lizard seeking a dry place in a rain forest. He shook his shoulders, and they shook back. There they stand, he thought: the object of my desire, my life, the woman of my dreams and her daughter. And there was no one to meet them. Where was Vallero? Luigi started to move to greet them, to offer them help with their bags, but pulled up abruptly when there appeared at the far corner of the depot the form of a large person emitting large puffs of frosty breath and swaying slightly in time with his heavy breathing. Vallero, the husband. *"A l'e neiru me' n'cruas,"* you're as drunk as a crow, muttered Luigi Suardi scornfully, in a vain effort to put himself on the same field with a rival he knew had the critical advantage of holy matrimony going for him.

"Thank you," said Maria as she smiled up into the kindly black face of the conductor. "Thank you so much." She somehow sensed that the man was unaccustomed to helping Interurban passengers with their baggage, as that was a service reserved for high-tipping First Class passengers on the trains that connected big cities. Maria took her purse out and searched in its depths for a coin, but was stopped when the conductor gently laid a large gloved hand over hers.

"That won't be necessary, he said in a deep voice that seemed to soften and round the words he spoke even before they passed his lips. Maria was accustomed to hearing a variety of dialects from Italy but had never before heard a black man speak. She liked the sound of his voice, whose unhurried style contrasted sharply with his obvious physical desire to get back on board the train. Only much later did Maria learn that her new home town had a history of violent racial conflict spawned by class warfare that pitted an autocratic mine-owner, Samuel M. Dalzell, against unionized coal miners influenced by radical immigrants, most of them from northern Italy, who agitated for the revolutionary political ideology of anarcho-syndicalism and printed an Italian-language paper, *L'Aurora.* The conflict had first erupted some twenty years before, when Danzell imported 200 blacks to break the back of a strike by the miners. Later, a mob of townspeople, agitated by alleged robberies attributed to black citizens and led by an Italian brass band, marched into an area known as the

Location where the town's black population was concentrated, and caused the residents to flee from their homes. There were several casualties, but the violence never approached the level reported by the Chicago press, whose overblown stories threatened to produce an all-out race war with a ripple effect far beyond the borders of Spring Valley.

Antonio Vallero had nearly forgotten the beauty of the wife he had left in Italy. As she stood looking along the station platform for the only human being she knew of in this strange new environment, the yellow light from the kerosene lantern cast a warm glow on her upturned face. Antonio was spellbound. Dear God, he thought, how could I have left this gorgeous creature? He lifted his hat to smooth his hair, ran his tongue over his teeth in an effort to remove the residual brown taste of grappa and pasta, straightened his overcoat and cleared his throat. Antonio wanted more than anything he had wanted in a long time to make a grand entrance worthy of this magnificent woman.

"Maria," he called, and extended his arms as he moved out from the shadows beside the depot. "Maria Roscio," and he hesitated before whispering his own name, her married name, "Vallero." The sound of his own name attributed to another person, his wife, this beautiful wife and mother, seemed unreal and got stuck in his throat. Maria recognized her legal husband with mixed feelings, but managed a smile. "You have come at last," said Vallero as he tried to hurry to her side only to trip over a broom handle lying on the platform, which caused him to lose his footing on the icy surface and fall backwards. Struggling to get up on one knee, Antonio cursed under his breath, *Cristu Santo na Madonna*, groaned over the loss of his moment and worse, his uttering a curse that would surely be regarded as an insult by the pious woman whom he had wanted so much to impress in a positive way.

She knew it was inappropriate, but there was no help for it: she had to look down on her husband and she had to laugh. It was a goodhearted laugh, but nevertheless, Antonio's pride, the most vulnerable part of any man, was wounded in a serious way. Rosa's giggle only half suppressed behind her mitten worsened the hurt. "Here, let me take your bags," was all he could say by way of making a civil gesture towards a woman he had been prepared to greet graciously, to worship, only moments before.

"Mama, who is this man?" asked Rosa.

"This man," said her mother sternly, "is your father. You know that, you silly goose, so stop your giggling and come along."

Antonio took their bags and led the distaff members of his family to a waiting horse-drawn buggy that took them to their new home, a ten minute drive from the station.

Once inside the two-room bungalow, Antonio lighted a kerosene lamp on the kitchen table and then made straight for the kitchen cupboard to extract a bottle of grappa and pour out half a tumbler, which he quaffed in a single gulp in a vain effort to regain the composure and upbeat feeling he had enjoyed playing cards with his buddies before leaving his dignity around his ankles on the railway station platform.

Maria lit the only other lamp in the house and used it to light the way into the bedroom, where she quickly went about moving all of her earthly possessions into a chest of drawers covered with chipped faded white paint and adorned on top with a scrap of yellow and red plaid oil cloth. The place reeked of cheap cigars, their persistent smell captured in the dingy curtains, soiled carpet and even the tattered bedspread. Maria moved to open the paned window to let in the fresh air craved by her body and soul. It was stuck, closed in an icy grip, and Maria, infuriated by the thought that the window had probably remained shut since autumn, gave it a mighty shove. Adrenaline driven by anger had given her strength far greater than could reasonably be expected in such a slight body, and the frozen window shattered under the impact of her assault.

Maria fell back on the bed and cried.

"Oh, God, forgive me," she sobbed, and let her tears wash away the unhappiness that suddenly overwhelmed her. The resolve that had carried her away from her childhood home, away from the musician she loved, to this strange cold, hard and dirty place, gave way to wrenching regret.

Antonio stood above his wife and laid his hand on her shoulder to give her comfort. Maria shuddered slightly, then put her hand on top of his, responding to the first adult sign of affection to be shown her in what seemed like an eternity. And he was, after all, her husband.

Vallero, too, experienced the feeling of love for his wife. But the warmth of her soft hand caused carnal desire to well up and triumph.

"No, please," pleaded Maria softly as Antonio grasped her breast. His breath was hot and came in short bursts. Her plea had an opposite effect on her husband and, frustrated by the intricacies of the buttons at the throat of her dress, Antonio grabbed the material and tore it down and away from her body, exposing one breast, its nipple hardened by the frigid cold in the room. This sight further inflamed the crazed desire of the man and he acted to exercise his conjugal rights, if necessary, by violent means. Suspenders released, pants lowered, her dress pulled upwards and used to gag her protests ....

The bedroom door hinges squeaked, and a small voice sounded.

"Mama?"

Maria Roscio Vallero threw her husband to the floor, and shouted a vulgar curse she had heard only once when her father had hurled it at an obnoxious foreman in the vineyards, "Va fate ciavar." Having thus invited her husband to do unto himself what he had just attempted to do to her, Maria ended for all practical intents and purposes her marriage to Antonio Vallero. A loud banging on the door startled both parties and broke through their embarrassed silence like an unexpected roll of thunder on a summer's evening weighted down with humidity.

"Hey, Tony, whatcha doin'?"

"Yeah, ya gonna leave us out in the cold?"

"The cards are gonna freeze together if we don't warm 'em up pretty soon."

"And listen, Tony, we got some fresh money to stir into the pot. New player straight from the old country."

Antonio Vallero grabbed his coat and hat, threw an unfocused, scornful look in the general direction of Maria, and shouted at the door:

"Hold on. I'll be there in a second. We can't play here tonight anyway. I'll just grab a few of my things...

"Never mind," said Maria evenly, her eyes locked on her former husband, the man who had assaulted her just moments before. "I'll put them all in a box and leave them outside the door at noon tomorrow. Adieu."

"Si," nodded Antonio. "Ciao."

CHAPTER 8

"This is the day that the Lord hath made," said Maria, as she looked out onto the sun-drenched landscape whose ash grey coat supplied by the four mines of Spring Valley had suddenly been replaced, for a splendid moment, by a verdant green cover, which warmed Maria's heart, mind and soul with a promise of hope and fulfillment tinged with melancholy as she thought of her mother and the home she had left, perhaps forever. "Let us rejoice and be glad within it," she concluded in a whisper. Her mother had blessed each morning with these words as soon as she got dressed and opened the door to let in the fresh air of a new day. It was her way of expressing gratitude for the gift of life, the ability to contemplate, however briefly, the wondrous world around her, regardless of circumstances, regardless of what joy or hardship, satisfaction or frustration the day might bring. The slag heap that rose up behind Mine #1 provided a landscape backdrop less pleasing to the eye than the grandiose Alps of her childhood, but the grass was the same color and so were the daffodils that had sprung up in little groups that passed for gardens around the front doors of the bungalows on the street that Maria had already come to think of as a real home for her family of two. It was Palm Sunday and Maria would take her Rosa to the little Church of the Immaculate Conception, which had become the centerpiece of their life after the final departure of Vallero left them to walk alone. It was at this church that Maria had made the acquaintance of the Lorentti's, Grande and Alice. This older couple, who had never been blessed with children, had done better than most of the northern Italian immigrants for that very reason. Without the consuming demands of children, they could devote more of their earnings, time and energies to getting ahead, building the American dream, getting rich. They had opened a small, checkered-tablecloth cafe that opened early and closed late to accommodate the appetites of both shifts at the nearby mine. Their ragged clientele was small in number but fiercely loyal, and the Lorentti's prospered within the limits imposed by the size of their business and the unpaid tabs that they permitted to pile up without comment to delinquent customers. Still, there was a very real void in their big hearts, which little Rosa came to fill.

In return, the Lorentti's needed desperately to have some help in the kitchen of their cafe, and Maria was only too happy to help. the nestegg supplied by her mother had nearly run out and if Maria failed to get some steady income, she would have had to go to work in the mines as a trapper (coal door-opener), a job usually handled by young boys, just to earn enough to pay for rent and groceries. But then, who would care for Rosa? Maria had heard that children who were taken into the pits with their mothers risked being adopted or, worse, made wards of the state.

Outside the church after Mass, Maria gave her daughter permission to run off and play cowboys-and-indians with some little people armed with palm fronds, and turned her face into the warm rays of the spring-empowered sunshine. She closed her eyes to let the warmth caress her high cheekbones and her throat. She took a deep breath and suddenly realized how much she had missed the sun during the seemingly endless winter months, how she had come to crave its special warmth.

"Maria."

Startled out of her reverie, Maria turned to the smiling face of Alice Lorentti. "Oh, Alice. I was just soaking up the spring, to store away some of it in case it goes away."

"Isn't it wonderful?"

"I think that this time, spring is really here to stay," said Grande in a tone of reassurance. "And by the way, Maria, I think Alice has something to propose, uh, suggest to you."

"Oh?" asked Maria, who had become comfortable with the Lorenttis, and grateful to them for giving her a job that would permit her to have her daughter in the cafe kitchen with her while she worked. Maria's benefactors had even secured a small couch where Rosa could take a nap in the afternoons at the cafe.

"Well, uh, I thought, I mean since your hus ... since Antonio Vallero has left ..."

"What my dear wife means to say," interjected Grande, "is that we have become acquainted with a very nice man we would like you to meet. He comes to church as often as possible, but early morning Mass is difficult for him."

"And why is that?" asked Maria in a sterner voice than she had intended.

"Well, you see, Maria," pleased Alice, "please don't be offended by our, um, suggestion. You see, he works all night, and ...

"In the mines?"

"No, no dear Maria. He is a musician and plays all night at the dance club."

"A musician, you say? What, uh, what does he play?" asked Maria, as her voice became pinched by a sudden flow of excitement rising from deep inside her.

"Why, he plays the accordion."

"Oh," exclaimed Maria, softly. She tried unsuccessfully to conceal her feelings of hope that the man was her secret love.

"Do you perhaps know this man?" asked Alice, with her understanding gaze turned on a suddenly silent Maria.

"No, of course not, Alice. How cold she possibly have met Luigi?"

"Luigi, you say?" asked Maria.

"Why, yes," said Grande, "Luigi Suardi is his name."

"We've invited him over for coffee this afternoon, interrupted his wife. "I do hope you'll be able to join us."

"Oh, I'd be delighted. Yes, thank you, Alice." Maria's heart was beating so fast that she feared the Lorenttis would be able to hear the sound, and she called for Rosa in a voice as loud as she could summon. Rosa came running, fearful that something was wrong because of the urgent tone in her mother's voice.

"Rosa, Mr. and Mrs. Lorentti have invited us to their house for some hot chocolate and cakes this afternoon. Is that not wonderful?"

"Oh, yes, Mama," squealed Rosa, whose appetite for sweets was enhanced by their nearly total absence from the spartan diet in her home.

Luigi Suardi had first met the Lorenttis at the dance hall where he performed. Grande was the lead tenor in a barbershop quartet that occasionally met at the hall to sing to the accompaniment of Luigi's accordion. Later, they got together at a special fund-raising pot luck dinner and sing-a-long at church. When the Lorenttis invited Luigi to their home, they expressed the hope that they would be able to introduce him to a lovely lady of their acquaintance by the name of Maria Vallero. She was a good Catholic woman, they said, who had only recently been abandoned by her husband.

"Did I know this man?" Luigi had asked, in hopes that it might be the one he hoped it would be.

"His Christian name is Antonio," said Grande, "Antonio Vallero, who has been in Spring Valley only a year or two."

Luigi realized in a flash of lightning that left him breathless: this had to be Antonio Vallero of Valperga and the wife he had left must be his Maria.

Luigi Suardi had never looked forward to anything as much as he looked forward to this meeting with the woman he had followed all the way to America without any real hope of ever getting close to. As his mind and body tossed and turned in the days before what he saw as a fateful reunion, Luigi was consumed by her imagined presence. And he wondered, during the brief periods when he was able to think of anything in the abstract, if the satisfaction he derived from his anticipation of meeting Maria could ever be exceeded.

The ache of anticipation suffered by Luigi for three days was telescoped into an electrically-charged period of three hours for Maria. It was a brief period of time stretched by desire to eternity, three hours that seemed too long to endure and yet too short to prep;are for a meeting she knew with intuitive certainty would be a turning point in her young life.

Maria took Rosa's hand, bid a cheerful adieu to the Lorenttis and moved off at an unusually rapid pace.

"Mama, why are you walking so fast," asked her daughter. "Are you in a big hurry to get home?"

"No, no, Rosa, I just want to get home before the rain comes down."

"What rain, Mama?"

"Well, don't you see those big black clouds up there, over the church steeple?"

"Yes, I do. But there is bright sunshine behind us. Do you think we'll get a big beautiful rainbow like yesterday."

"Oh, yes, I'm quite sure of that."

Maria smiled down at the bobbing head of her daughter and wondered why it was that the pace of little children always contradicted the tempo set by their parents. On a leisurely stroll in the park, for example. Rosa always ran at full speed, without any particular destination in mind for more than a few seconds at a time. It just seemed to be of great importance to reach the oak tree and hide behind it for a moment, and then to race over to a picnic table where a fallen acorn lay waiting to be discovered. And now, when her mother was obviously in a hurry to get home, Rosa's progress was impeded by a dozen distractions: the cracks in the sidewalk to be avoided, a brightly colored bird demanding attention by noisily hammering at the gnarled trunk of an old chestnut tree, the fast moving clouds whose shapes had to be identified with creatures only recently imprinted on the sponge-like mind of a curious four-year-old child.

As Maria brushed out her thick tresses from the tight braids she felt were required for Sunday Mass, time slowed to Rosa's molasses-in-January tempo. Repeated looks at the watch her mother had given her for her trip to the New World failed to speed the hands that seemed frozen by some irascible power. She must get busy, thought Maria. That always made time pass quickly. But what was there to busy herself with? She had already changed out of her black dress reserved for church and into a charmingly low-cut dark green satin frock. Rosa was cleaned and groomed and placed on a kitchen chair to preserve the pretty picture. Maria sat in a chair opposite her daughter, sighed deeply and smiled.

"I think you are happy, Mama."

"Yes, I am. How can you tell?"

"Because your eyes tell me you are happy."

"Well, you are absolutely right, my dear Rosa. And you are absolutely the most observant child in the world. Here, give me a hug," said Maria as she jumped from her chair and sprang around the table into her daughter's outstretched arms.

The warm embrace of mother and daughter was interrupted by the raucous sound of the hand-operated brass horn mounted on the side of the Model T Ford driven into the driveway by Grande Lorentti. Only then did Maria pull back the lacey curtain to reveal the heavy clouds just starting to release their raindrops and first felt, then heard the drumroll of thunder that signaled the violent, irreconcilable struggle of the elements to reach equilibrium on a typical midwestern summer afternoon. Her eyes widened. Never had she seen nature in such turmoil. She was awestruck but unafraid; rather, the electricity seemed to invest her already elevated sense of anticipated pleasure with added excitement. She shivered slightly as she waved to Lorentti, grabbed an umbrella with one hand and Rosa with the other, and bounced out the door to meet the future head on.

Lorentti acknowledge Maria's expressed appreciation of his new car with a huge smile that spread across his broad face from ear to ear.

"Yes, I like the car myself, even though I would have preferred a brighter color."

"Didn't you have a choice in the matter," queried Maria with her eyebrows raised high in a tone of feminine ignorance of such a masculine business.

"Oh, yes, I certainly did," said Grande Lorentti with a chuckle building in his throat. "Henry Ford, of whom you will recall I have spoken before, has announced last year that his customer could have any color they wanted, provided it was black."

"I see," said Maria, as she helped her daughter into the front seat and then let Grande take her gloved hand and guide her into the seat next to the window. "I thought you admired this Mr. Ford. Now you make him sound like some sort of a tyrant."

"No, to the contrary," said Grande as he moved around to the driver's side of the shiny new vehicle. "I do admire the man who built my beautiful new car, and who just recently shared ten million dollars of his company's profits with his coworkers. "You see, my dear," said Lorentti with a jovial toss of his white-thatched head, Mr. Ford wants his workers to be able to afford to buy the cars they are making. He is what you might call a truly American industrialist, an entrepreneur with a *heart* as well as a head."

"Oh, does he give his cars away?" asked Maria with a mischievous giggle, as Lorentti struggled with the levers protruding from the steering column that had to be set in a certain position for the car to start.

"No, far from it," said Lorentti as he walked to the front of the engine and inserted the starter crank in its recess. "But he's guided by what I call enlightened self interest." On the third crank the engine started with a thunderous howl that startled the passengers on their first ride in a passenger car. The driver quickly climbed into his seat and adjusted the levers in a way that calmed the noise and movement of the engine.

"And how does it work, this 'enlightened self interest,'" asked Maria in a serious tone free of sarcasm.

Lorentti looked into his passenger's steady gaze and realized that for all her obviously female attributes and her occasionally coquettish mannerisms, this woman had a strong and inquiring mind. She actually wanted to know more about Henry Ford.

"Well," said Lorentti as he sought to lower the volume of his resonant voice to the reduced noise level of the Model T's engine, "Henry Ford understands that by winning the support and loyalty of his workers, even if it costs him money in the short run, will make him more money in the long run.

"Is that why he decided to give his workers a minimum daily wage? Five dollars a day, was it not?

"Exactly," said Lorentti, noticeably impressed by Maria's knowledge of Ford's recent action that had infuriated the other automakers. You see, this is quite different from the *patroni* who do everything they can to make as much money as possible in the shortest possible time, powerful men who view their workers as merely pawns in a gigantic chess game played by the so-called 'captains of industry' in the cozy confines of their gentlemen clubs and aboard their luxury yachts."

"The robber barons," said Maria, who had only recently read the word in an Italian-language flyer distributed in miners' neighborhoods by anarchists in the mines. These rawboned, heavily-bearded miners, most of them from northern Italy proudly accepted the popular epithet of "Wobbly" coined from the IWW acronym of their trade union organization, the Industrial Workers of the World. They refused, however, to silently accept as some sort of natural economic law the notion that their subsistence level wages paid for mining coal eleven hours a day in sunless pits was a non-negotiable condition fixed by the unchangeable laws of supply and demand at the point on a sheet of graph paper where the supply of workers intersected with the demand for their labor.

Grande Lorentti both liked and feared the Wobblies.

He sympathized with their opposition to low wages paid by the mine owners, inhuman working conditions in the mines and the institution of the company store, which owners used to turn hard working miners and their families into little more than chattels for life. But Lorentti could not accept the anarchists' call for violent means as the only possible way to achieve their revolutionary ends.

In discussing politics with Maria at a church social in early spring, Lorentti, who enjoyed acting as this young woman's mentor, had summed up his views in a way that she would long remember. "I agree with the miners' grievances as you know," he had said. "But I simply cannot believe that violence can ever be used to achieve social justice. Noble purposes can never be achieved by bloodshed."

"But what can be done to help these workers?" she had asked. "Maybe more people like Henry Ford," answered Lorentti. More powerful men blessed with compassion.

Luigi was uncomfortably seated in the Lorentti's parlor when Maria and Rosa arrived. As he rose to address the woman he had for so long dreamed to meet, his rain-soaked shoes emitted an undignified squishing sound, which made both Luigi and Maria look down and then look into each other's eyes, which led through embarrassment to a giggling recognition of the humor in the situation. The ice was broken. Luigi then acknowledged his formal introduction to Maria with a deep bow. He took Maria's tiny hand in his and caressed it with a lingering, gentle kiss. Maria looked down on her admirer and saw her future.

Rosa, who had remained quiet during the introductions, suddenly shouted as she pointed to the curtained bay window: "Look, just look at that rainbow. Is it not wonderful?"

"Yes, Rosa," said her mother. "It is a beautiful sight."

"A beautiful sight, indeed," whispered Luigi, without taking his coal black eyes from Maria.

"And now let us raise our glasses to this fine rainbow," said Grande, as he finished pouring the red wine from a fine cut crystal decanter into four crystal glasses.

"Salute to the beauty of God's nature, to our great country of America and to our wonderful friendship."

"And salute," Maria spoke in a strong voice that halted the ascent of the glasses in mid-air, "to Henry Ford."

Without knowing what she was talking about, but impressed by the conviction in her voice, Luigi Suardi looked into Maria's eyes and smiled. "To Henry Ford," he said, and touched her glass with his won, gently.

CHAPTER 9

As the social small talk started to run out, Luigi brought out his accordion and played some songs from Italy that lifted the company to an unexpectedly festive mood. Soon they were like family, singing and humming along with Luigi's strong baritone. The musician concluded his performance by singing with a warmth impossible to conceal Eduardo di Capua's romantic ballad Maria, Mari. He sang the chorus first in Italian and then in English –

> *Ah, Mari, ah, Mari,*
> *All the sleep I am losing for thee!*
> *Now, let me rest,*
> *for a moment asleep on they breast –*

and the subject of the serenade felt the blood moving to her head so fast that all efforts to forestall the blush were doomed, and Maria gave up the effort with a self-conscious half-smile.

Suddenly, Maria broke the silence to announce that it was perhaps time to leave, because it was getting late for Rosa, who spluttered a protest through a mouthful of cake to the amusement of all. With a graceful wave of her finger, Maria reminded her daughter that decisions of this nature were never to be questioned by little people. Grande Lorentti offered to drive his guests home, but before Maria could respond, Luigi said that he would be happy to escort the ladies home if they didn't mind walking. Maria accepted his offer over Rosa's pleas to get another ride in her "uncle's" new auto, and the three set out on foot. Maria's shoes were unsuited for walking any distance, but the blisters forming on her feet went unnoticed as did the mud puddles that drew Rosa to them like magnets. Sensing Maria's displeasure with her daughter's tomboyish behavior, Luigi suddenly took the little girl's hand to guide her around a particularly large puddle. While pretending not to see it, Maria was surprised, and secretly pleased by the way in which her generally shy daughter had accepted the older man's hand. Then it happened, as suddenly and impulsively as a child's smile: Rose brought Luigi's hand around to touch her mother's, as she skipped behind and took Maria's left hand in her own. Storm clouds gathered overhead and caused the silent, smiling three to quicken their pace to get inside Maria's bungalow. Only when she reached into her purse for the latchkey did Maria take her hand from the warm embrace of Luigi's.

"I must apologize for this place. I hope to be able to get a better home one day. This place, I call it a dump, was rented by my husband, who, uh, who has left me, but why do I go on like this. Forgive ..."

"There is nothing to forgive Signora Vallero. May I call you Maria?"

"Please do so."

"You see, the Lorenttis have told me the sad story of how your husband mistreated you, Maria, and how you had to throw him out. And ..."

"Yes?" By this time Maria was hanging on Luigi's every word and wanted him to continue. To speak in his wonderful voice, to go on making what had become music to her ears.

"Yes, well, you see I am so sympathetic to your situation. I mean ever since I met you at your wedding and later saw you on the ship ..."

"So, it was you on the Colombo?"

"Yes, I just can't help feeling that, well, I mean it just seems that we were somehow meant to be brought together by some sort of greater power, call it fate or what ..."

Luigi's reflection was interrupted by a bolt of lightning that flashed through the room as thunder simultaneously shook the floor beneath them. Luigi moved quickly to take hold of the person he now thought of as *his* Maria, to protect her from the storm raging outside and from men such as the person she had been made to marry. He felt her quietly trembling in his embrace, and he heard her voice whisper, "Thank you, Luigi," before she slid away to hug and comfort her daughter, who had burst into tears, out of fear for the thunder.

As much as Maria was comforted and made to feel whole within the embrace of *her* Luigi, she felt no particular need to be protected by anyone from the violence of natural elements or man-made abuse. She only knew with a certainty that went beyond rational thought and the borders of fear that the awesome sound and fury of thunder and lightning signalled a wondrous moment in her lie. She was always receptive to such supernatural signals, whether they arrived wrapped in grey clouds of fear and foreboding or, as now, on the soaring wings of promised pleasure.

Luigi sensed the critical importance of Rosa in the life of her mother, and hence in his winning the love of Maria for the long term. And the long term was what he wanted, needed and knew to be the only kind of relationship Maria would accept. This was a new and different feeling. Luigi Suardi had known short-term stints with either conspicuously hot young admirers, who doubled the beat of music in movements that suggested a hurried effort to get undressed for his pleasure, or languorous matrons whose eyes and deliberately measured movements promised sensual fulfillment that could most effectively be provided by experienced moves accelerated by fear of dying.

Maria was not of Luigi's known world, which he had come to realize was as flat and thin as the earth was once believed to be. Maria was very much alive, real. This face was established by the warmth she breathed into their brief embrace. But for some reason Luigi sensed that this woman who had occupied his psyche for so long was as much an ideal created by ancient philosophers and shaped by modern artists, as she was a human being like himself enslaved by randomly ordered and habitually disobedient emotions. Luigi picked up his accordion and played.

Maria, Mari!, he sang with his gaze focused on Rosa, "*Quanta Suon-no che per-do pe te; Fam m'ad due mi Oj Mari ...*" Mother and daughter smiled first at this stranger who had come from nowhere to be a part of their little family, then at each other.

Maria broke the passionate silence.

"Rosa, what poor hostesses we are. We must prepare a little supper for our guest."

"A guest?" asked Rosa.

"Now you hurry along and set the table."

As Rosa moved slowly to fetch plates from the cupboard, Luigi strapped on his accordion and began to play a sprightly child's song, which he knew would endear him to Rosa and he knew with equal certainty would endear him to her mother. Presto! Rosa's little feet suddenly came to life, moving in time with the music as she danced to the cupboard, her curls happily bouncing on her bobbing head. Maria recognized the tune and moved to the wood stove with a swaying motion that gave her prosaic kitchen errand the graceful appearance of a ballet dance. She lifted the heavy iron plate as if it were weightless with one hand while the other hand swept a match stick from a ledge overhead and lit the kindling in the stove opening in a continuous motion. Maria's impromptu operetta performance concluded with a tiny bow and a smile from below the cascade of dark hair falling over her cocked head, which conveyed her unbridled happiness to the musician who inspired it. Luigi replied with a spontaneous smile of appreciation and a nod of encouragement.

From a tiny icebox, Maria removed a ball of chilled *polenta*, a northern Italian staple that even the poorest family could put on the table accompanied by whatever meat, fish or cheese was available. In the worst of times a slice of the cold corn meal mush that dated back to the millet and wheat dish that had been eaten by Roman soldiers in th field in ancient times, could be anointed with olive oil and rubbed against an anchovy for flavor. Going a step higher on the gastronomical scale, Maria fried the corn meal slices in a mixture of butter and olive oil and served them up with pieces of local Funtina cheese she bought at the nearby delicatessen whose proprietor extended credit in exchange for a smile. She then snipped some sprigs of fresh Lemon Basil from a dish on the window sill above the kitchen sink, rinsed coal dust from the herbs and carefully positioned each piece of bright green garnish atop the polenta, magically transforming the peasant fare into the main course of a royal banquet.

While continuing to play his children's concert, Luigi grew fascinated by the way Maria moved about the small room. She seemed to repeal the law of gravity as her feet glided in their purposeful course without any apparent contact with the wooden floor. At the grey metallic sink she worked the pump handle in time with Luigi's music to bring up just enough water to cleanse her basil bouquet, then playfully shook the excess over the head of her daughter, who squealed and fled into the bedroom. Luigi wanted to freeze the scene, to keep the beauty of the mother-child tableau on his mind's stage forever.

At that moment, Maria turned to face the man. Their eyes locked in the recognition of an emotion that joined them together and carried them above and beyond any known feeling to an unknown and unknowable future. The accordion went silent. They were in love.

"I'm hungry," said a small voice from the corner of the room. Rosa's mundane statement of fact released Maria and Luigi from their shared moment above and beyond the real world in which people had to eat and work and sleep and make love, and eventually, die. They both felt relieved. Now that their love was established, they could return to reality with the hope and grace that can never be achieved in the absence of love.

❖❖❖

The music stopped, and Maria's strong contralto voice reached the ears of the three men standing outside in the shadows of the darkening street.

... and these your gifts which we are about to receive from your goodness, through Christ our Lord. Amen."

"Si, amen, you *strega*," said the smaller of the coal-blackened miners. "Notice how he lets the woman say grace."

"Dio faus," cursed another, "that squeeze box player must have *bale quadre*."

"Or no balls at all," muttered the larger miner, which triggered a guttural outburst of raucous laughter punctuated by scornful epithets the men took turns in shouting to the blue-black sky: *tabalore, turlupupu, balengo*.

"So, let's go get the son of a whore who's won the witch's heart and made her drive our good friend out of town," said the small one.

"Hold on," said the big man, one of the few Italian anarchists to remain in Spring Valley after their violent confrontation with black miners in 1895. Speaking sarcastically in the highly educated form of speech generally attributed by the workers to members of the ruling class, he proclaimed: "While you are quite correct in your analysis of the situation, and you are clearly justified in your call for vengeance to restore the good name of our comrade, Senor Vallero, we must act in a rational manner that will not cause an alarm that could bring the police to the aid of our enemy."

"Quite right," the small one said, picking up on the mocking style of his larger and older companion. "I propose that we repair to Delmargo's saloon for further consultation, and the adoption of a plan of action." And the three marched off to the nearby oasis.

It was nearly impossible for Luigi to eat the polenta, as the food kept getting hung up on the blockage caused by his emotional preoccupation with his hostess. The dim light of the candles, which served as the only source of illumination in the place, only enhanced Maria's beauty, and made Luigi's ingestive attempts more difficult.

"I must get my daughter to bed," she said, and only then did Luigi notice that Maria had failed to eat any of the tasty dish set before her. Instead, she had covered her lack of appetite by taking some spoonsful of the polenta from her dish and giving them to her always hungry daughter.

"Then I must go, my dear ..." The phrase of endearment slipped out unintentionally, and Luigi showed his embarrassment. "That is, I hope I have not overstayed my welcome."

"Not at all, said Maria, as she moved behind Rosa's chair and put her arms on the thin shoulders of her sleepy daughter. "I only hope you will call again, soon, that is, I hope you will call again," casting a quick glance at Luigi's half finished plate, "when I shall have a better meal for you."

"Maria, please do not apologize. You, uh, the meal, it was absolutely wonderful." Luigi was caught in a riptide produced by the conventional demand for a polite withdrawal and the flooding emotional urge to take her in his arms. The shared dilemma was resolved when Maria smiled and gently lowered her eyes from Luigi to her daughter, at the same time extending her tiny hand. Luigi took a half-step towards them and after kissing her hand with a warmth she had never before felt, he turned to leave. At the door, he had to clear his throat before he looked back and said in a voice the strength of which came as a surprise to both man and woman: "Arrivederci, my dear Maria."

Maria. The song kept humming by itself at a point just below her throat as the happy woman lay down in bed beside the little girl who would always be her baby, though she was growing so rapidly that the bedtime snuggle at the wondrous twilight time between consciousness and sleep would soon be ended. Exhausted by the crowded day, Rosa had fallen asleep as she concluded her prayers, "... I pray the Lord my soul to keep."

Maria lay still, totally relaxed, experiencing a new state of consciousness above and beyond the governing operation of her senses, filled with the love of her daughter and the man whose presence had transformed her life, raised it to a higher level. It was then that she saw as clearly as if she were standing at the scene, three men in sooty clothes attack her Luigi. A huge man struck him flush in the face and knocked him down in the muddy gutter. Luigi raised his hands to shield his face and the little bully took a running start and kicked him in the back. And when Luigi raised himself to kneel on all fours, the third assailant kicked him back down with a blow to the side of his head.

Maria's senses turned on in a flash and she actually felt the blows falling on Luigi. She ran out the door without consciously opening it, and sprinted down the street to the rescue of her beloved. His attackers were quickly driven away by a blood-curling scream that belied her small stature.

With that inexplicable surge of strength that has been known to enable average size persons to lift cars from the bodies of children pinned under them, Maria lifted her Luigi to his feet and half carried, half dragged him two blocks to her home. After she tenderly cleaned his wounds, removed his mud-spattered clothes and lay him under a woolen blanket on the sofa, Luigi opened his eyes, looked at Maria and smiled weakly in gratitude, then looked around the room. "My accordion," he stammered through bloodcrusted lips, "where is ..." Maria gently covered his mouth, nodded to assure him that she understood, and ran back to the scene of the assault to recover the instrument that the bullies had smashed and thrown into the gutter.

When she re-entered the tiny living room, which was now bathed in moonlight, she saw Luigi propped up on one arm.

"Did they, is it ...?

"It's all right. Your accordion can be repaired," she lied in consolation.

"Thank God," whispered a man of sensibility who felt he had traveled from the sublime heights of heaven to the depths of the blackest hell and back again in the arms of his beloved, who had slipped under the cover to lay beside him. He felt the glowing warmth of her body and only then realized that she had somehow managed to get undressed. Her bosom lifted and he felt the hardened nipple touch his chin. Maria, whose only physical contact with a man had been encased in a paralyzing cold of fear and resistance, suddenly convulsed as she gave herself unconditionally to this man. Luigi, whose sexual contacts with women were as shallow and self-serving as they were frequent, now felt transported to an earlier unknown and higher level of experience with this unique woman, his beloved.

CHAPTER 10

In the autumn of 1916, President Wilson signed into law a bill requiring an eight-hour day for railway workers and assured a gathering of cheering suffragettes that women would get to vote "in a little while." Wilson was elected to a second term in the White House and Jeanette Rankin, a Montana Republican, became the first woman to win a seat in the U.S. Congress; 318 mostly "foreign born" striking coal miner members of the I.W.W. were arrested when they tried to hold a secret meeting in Old Forge, Pennsylvania; Standard Oil stock hit $2,000 per share, making John D. Rockefeller a billionaire; Ford produced 508,000 cars and a profit of $60 million, much of which would go for higher salaries and profit-sharing with the workforce; tanks proved decisive in a successful Allied drive on the Somme front, while German U-boats stepped up their attacks on merchant shipping along the U.S. coast; and, Mrs. Margaret Sanger, who earlier served

30 days in jail for opening a birth control clinic, continued her campaign to spur social progress by limiting the size of families.

Maria read the news in Spring Valley Evening Gazette and, occasionally, the Italian-language *L'Aurora*, whose circulation of 3,000 copies in a city with 7,000 inhabitants was more a reflection of its linguistic appeal than that of its anarchist political line. In addition, Maria frequently listened to new reports on a radio owned by her neighbor. But none of the tumultuous events of the time, not even the battles between Italian and Austrian forces not far from her mother's home, could distract Maria from her determined effort to both nurture her relationship with Luigi Suardi and to put it on a footing sanctified by both man-made law and the moral demands of her religion.

While she had no doubts that Luigi intended to remain faithful to her alone, Maria knew that she must attend to her lover's sexual needs (and, coincidentally, her own) without overstepping the outer limits of the rules of her Church. On more than one occasion when they were together, Luigi looked on attractive women in a way that made Maria sick with jealousy. While walking along the banks of Spring Creek one late fall day, she had caught him feasting his eyes on a voluptuous blonde seated on a park bench. "She is quite beautiful, don't you think," Maria had asked him in a friendly conversational tone. His hurried response – "Oh, what lady do you mean?" – only strengthened her resolve to satisfy his carnal needs, lest they lead him astray, whether by his own conscious desire, which she doubted would happen, or by the wiles of another woman, which she believed could and most likely would happen to a monastic Luigi. Lest he misunderstand her drawing the line between what was acceptable and what was forbidden, Maria told Luigi that she could never perform sex in the conventional manner, with his entrance into her in a way that could create new life, before they were united as husband and wife in the sacrament of holy matrimony administered by the Church. And so the lovers tacitly agreed to satisfy their irrepressible sexual needs in a limited way until they could be wed.

Meanwhile, Maria wrote to her mother describing her heaven-sent meeting with Luigi as well as her ill-treatment at the hands of her husband. Maria implored Giovanna Roscio to come to her assistance by somehow securing an annulment of her marriage to Vallero so that she could marry Luigi. This was accomplished within a few months as a result of the intercession of Fr. Pietro following the delivery to him of a substantial "gift to the poor," which Giovanna was able to raise through her own labors and gifts from her friends and neighbors.

Immediately after the awful night of Luigi's beating, Maria set out to get a larger dwelling that would enable her to operate a boarding house, the demand for which had skyrocketed with the hiring of new miners to satisfy the burgeoning demands for the primary fuel used by the awakening American industrial giant. With financial help in the form of a long-term, low interest loan given her by the Lorenttis, Maria became an innkeeper entrepreneur. This move brought in funds and provided a place for Luigi to live under the same roof with Maria. Their tiptoed nocturnal visits were now kept within four walls, screened from the salacious view of outsiders.

❖❖❖

In the autumn of 1917, Bolsheviks infiltrated the demoralized Russian army, seized power in a coup d'etat under slogans keyed to popular demands for bread and peace; American forces singing George M. Cohan's smash hit, *Over There*, moved into the mud- and blood-soaked front line trenches in France; the German spy Mata Hari was executed; and, nearly half a million Italian soldiers were taken prisoner or deserted their demoralized regiments in northern Italy. Maria took note of these events, which provided a curious mix of uplifting exhilaration tinged with a gray cloud of foreboding.

The outside world came to a complete standstill, however, on the day that Luigi and Maria appeared at the altar of the Church of the Immaculate Conception to join their lives in holy matrimony. In an unusually sunny Saturday, when even the pervasive clouds of smoke and coal dust from the mines took a day off, Maria and Luigi chose to speak their vows in the English language. The Italian-American priest who presided at the ceremony also complemented his memorized liturgical Latin with Biblical quotations delivered in heavily accented English.

"From Ecclesiasticus, Chapter 26: Happy the husband of a good wife; twice lengthened are his days; a worthy wife brings joy to her husband, peaceful and full is his life," recited the priest with his dark eyes fastened on the beautiful bride kneeling before him.

And then, turning to the groom, "Husbands love your wives, just as Christ loved the Church, and delivered himself for her, that he might sanctify her by cleansing her in the bath of water ..." Maria kept her eyes on her man. "Even so ought husbands to love their wives as their own bodies." A smile played at the corners of Maria's mouth, and she thought that freed of even marginal guilt feelings, she would now love her man with all her heart, mind and soul ... and, yes, with all her body, too.

Kneeling behind her mother was eight-year-old Rosa, dressed in a white gown stitched by Maria, holding a bouquet of hand-picked chrysanthemums. The Lorenttis dressed in their Sunday best were in a front pew. And all eight of the miners living at Maria's boarding house, were seated at the back of the church lest their ill-clad appearance be an embarrassment to the bridal couple.

The Lorenttis had offered to host the wedding reception at their home, but Maria politely insisted that the celebration be held at her house on the ostensible grounds that Alice and Grande had already gone to too much trouble and expense on her behalf. In reality, Maria wanted, indeed needed, to celebrate her wedding in her own home with her beloved husband and daughter, and with the miners who lived under the same roof, for whom she had developed both sympathy and respect. This she demonstrated by dancing with each and every one of them, sharing her happiness and lighting their darkened lives with a brief burst of pure, warming sunshine.

After the miners left for the Spring Valley Coal Company's Mine No. 2, and an exhausted Rosa was tucked into her new bed in the room formerly used by Luigi, Maria took Luigi by the hand and let him lead her upstairs to their nuptial bed in her room that she had decorated with flowers, candles and rose-scented potpourri.

Now their relationship was liberated from even the slightest chance of being considered adulterous. Gone was the limitation imposed by Maria to prevent their lovemaking from being stigmatized as a mortal sin. Never again would their love have to be hidden or restricted, but would be as openly wholesome as two bodies joined together, now and forever. The two opened their eyes and looked all the way into each other's souls without any physical movement to jar the magical beauty of the moment. Time stood still until both man and woman moved, at first slowly and then with a gradually accelerated tempo. His thrust caused her to rise up to meet him and then nearly lost contact before they came

together again, and again, at closer intervals, until ...
Maria heaved her hips, and moaned in ecstacy as she
received her lover husband, who came into her with his
entire being, leaving him with nothing but everything.

According to the theorem empirically tested and
verified in Italian bedrooms down through the ages, the
number of times a couple makes love during their first
year of their marriage will always exceed the total number of conjugal events during the remainder of their
union. The method for proving this law of the bedroom
is simple, inexpensive and as infallible as the word of the
Pope. The equipment consists of a container, preferably
made of glass, such as a Mason jar, and a bag of beans –
or pebbles for those who cannot bear to see food wasted.
Starting on the wedding night, each sexual union is
recorded by depositing a single bean into the jar. After
the first anniversary, each act of lovemaking is celebrat-
ed by the removal of a bean. The jar will never be emptied.

In the early autumn of 1918, on the first anniversary
of the marriage of Luigi and Maria Suardi, the multicul-
tural fabric of the Austro-Hungarian Empire began to
unravel; Allied forces drove the Kaiser's troops from
French soil; and, several employers suggested that it was
the patriotic duty of more than a million women
employed in war industries to leave their jobs as soon as
men return from the war.

Maria lit the kerosene lamp on the dining table and
asked her husband, who had just returned from the nearby dance hall, to join her for a glass of wine. This was an
unusual change in the couple's routine and Luigi sensed
that his wife had something on her mind of greater

importance than going to bed.

"Salut," said Maria as she raised her glass. "Salut," responded her husband. "Salut to all three of us," she continued in a matter of fact tone.

"What?" spluttered Luigi, with red wine spattering the clear glass chimney on the lamp in front of him. "Trei?"

"Trei, si."

Luigi jumped up and held the shoulders of his seated wife, kissed her hair and forehead over and over between expressions of joy with the news of his becoming a father. First-time fathers, it seemed, always treated the expectant mother as if she were suddenly reconstructed of a fragile material that might break if touched. And any expression of sexual desire, even a kiss on the lips, seemed somehow profane.

"I'm so pleased," said Maria softly, "and I'm happy that you're pleased, too."

The couple emptied their glasses in silence filled to overflowing as the news sank in. Luigi held the small hand of his young wife, who finally spoke in a voice both soft and yet forcefully resonant.

"Yes, it is wonderful that God has blessed us with a new life, my dear Luigi."

"What shall we call him ... or, uh, her?

"We have plenty of time to make that decision." But we first have to answer several practical questions."

"Yes, of course," said Luigi, not having the slightest idea what these questions might be, since he never interfered with his wife's management of the family's finances.

Maria outlined the problems that Suardi faced: Luigi's income from his playing in dance clubs and saloons, already reduced by payments on his new accordion, would soon be eliminated by the 18th Amendment to the Constitution. And Maria was strictly opposed to her husband's working in the illegal speakeasies that were being organized throughout the county to circumvent Prohibition. Operating the boarding house, including the preparation of two meals and packing lunch pails for the eight boarders was all Maria could handle. Maria finished her summary of the family's finances with one inescapable conclusion: more income would have to be raised somehow to pay overdue bills at the company grocery store and keep up with the mortgage payments.

"I could always to go work in the mines," said Luigi. "I hear they're paying a dollar an hour."

Maria took her husband's hands, smiled and shook her head slowly. "My dear Luigi. You would do this for me?"

"Yes, my beautiful Maria," he whispered into her ear, and then waited in vain for her to talk him out of his brave offer.

"Very well, I don't like it, but I guess it's the only way we can avoid charity or bankruptcy, or both," she said. "I'll pack an extra meal when our miners leave for the pits tonight. Go now and get some rest."

Luigi went to bed and tried but failed to sleep. He was stimulated both by the fear of working in the place with the bullies who had given him such a terrible beating and by the exhilaration of his own courage in facing up to this, the greatest challenge of his life.

Luigi Suardi's work in No. 2 mine lasted one week. His enemies, Vallero's buddies, were never a problem. When he first stepped off the elevator at the rumbling end of its 300-foot descent into the black ground, the larger of the bullies looked at him, squinted his eyes in disbelief and then nodded to Luigi with a look that conveyed respect. Buoyed by this unexpected encounter – he had anticipated meeting the huge man in a darkened corner of the mine where he would receive another beating – Luigi smiled and slowly lifted his right arm to give his tormentor a thumbs-up salute. That was the only positive happening in a week of clanging noise amplified by the agonized silence of the miners, whose fatigue and surrender to a lifetime of physical toil was reflected in their weary eyes. Eyes from which the light of hope had been extinguished, permanently. For the first few days underground, Luigi had successfully avoided swinging a pickaxe, but when it came his turn to attack the five-foot thick coal seam, he fought a losing battle. Blood oozed from sores that quickly replaced blisters on both palms and dropped from his sweaty arms on the black floor. A fellow miner, one of Maria's boarders, saw what was happening and tried to help Luigi.

"Here, let me help," he said in a low voice.

"First off, you've got to wrap your hands, because the blood will make the handle slip around and before you know it, you'll be hitting the seam with the flat side of the pick. And that ain't gonna cut any coal loose. Know what I mean?"

"Yes, I guess you're right," grunted Luigi through clenched teeth. Whereupon, he took his handkerchief from his hip pocket and let the helpful miner wrap his bleeding right hand.

The miner then picked up the pickaxe and from his kneeling position took a hefty cut into the shiny black face of the tunnel wall. He pulled back and a huge chunk broke out and fell to the floor.

"Ya see how to do it, man?" And without waiting for an answer, he took another swing at the wall. "You gotta make the pick work with you, let its weight be part of your muscle. The way you been hackin' at it, only half of your strength is goin' with the pick and the other half is goin' against it. It's a sort of a rhythm you gotta get into. So that you and the pick are one, single piece a machinery. Here, now try to do like I said."

Luigi took the pick handle and gave a mighty swing

to little effect. "I guess I just don't get it," he said. "I understand what you're saying, and I understand how I should swing this damned thing, but somehow I just can't seem to get into a rhythm like you do."

Maria rushed out to meet Luigi on the stoop as he returned with the boarders at noon. He was on the verge of tears, more from embarrassment than pain, as he let Maria lead him to their bedroom where she cleaned and bandaged his bleeding hands and spoon-fed him the polenta and grilled bell peppers with Bagna Cauda sauce, which she had spent much of the morning preparing. She took the empty bowl downstairs and, with Rosa's help served dinner to the miners who paid their respects to Maria and her husband with their silence. All but the youngest of them rounded off their main meal with a shot of grappa. The clear liquid was poured into small cups from a half-liter carafe formed from the same pottery as the cups that stood on a sideboard behind the dinner table. According to a medically untested but widely-held belief in the highlands of northern Italy, grappa, aka "white mule," serves as an incomparable aid to the stimulation of essential digestive juices and is, therefore, the best, and possibly the only healthy way to complete a dinner.

After the miners were served, their spokesman, the one who tried to instruct Luigi in the use of a pickaxe, signalled to Maria to join him outside. "I am sorry to tell you, Signora," he confided in hushed words, "but your husband ..." He turned his palms upwards, and Maria nodded her understanding. "I tried to help," he continued, but he is, well, you know, he is a fine musician."

"I understand, and I thank you for your help."

Maria then took a cup of grappa upstairs and held it to her man's lips. He drank the whole cup in one gulp while she took off her apron and got into bed beside him. Then, much to the surprise of his wonderful wife, Luigi laughed out loud. "What's funny?" she asked, as she smiled in amazement and relief to find that Luigi could manage laughter at a time like this. "Well, you see, I don't really think that I was meant to be a miner ..." "No, my darling man, I know," said Maria who was now chuckling with him. "What happened?" Her curiosity was too much to bear. "Tell me. Now." But his laughter continued. "Tell me or I'm going to leave this bed. Now!" "All right," said Luigi, "I'll tell you." Finally, after the strain of controlling his outburst brought tears to his eyes, Luigi told of his experience.

"You see, my dear lady, this old musician you have chosen to marry – God only knows why ...

"Come now, Luigi, tell me what happened."

"Well, you see nobody told me not to do it," and he had to stop to catch his breath and emit another chuckle.

"To do what, to do what?"

"To smoke a cigar down there."

"You lit a cigar in the mine?" asked Maria.

"Well, not quite, my dear. You see before I could get the match to my little butt of a cigar there was a little butt of an explosion!" Whereupon they both joined in laughter.

"Didn't they tell you," he asked.

"No, no one told me," said Maria as she took off the rest of her clothing. "Let's go back to Italia," she whispered as she moved on top of him. "Si," he groaned, as she gently moved downwards. Having settled that matter, they made tender and passionate love right there in a sun-filled bedroom, for what seemed an eternity.

CHAPTER 11

Winter struck suddenly with icy blasts of wind whipping across the Illinois River and swirling down the tunnel created by slag heaps alongside Spring Creek. White blankets of snow were quickly transformed on contact with the warm earth into heaps of grey slush that covered the landscape and turned the streets into rutted waterways enjoyed by only the very youngest of the townspeople, who were irresistibly attracted to slush and puddles as iron dust is drawn to a magnet. It was in this dismal setting that Luigi and Maria Suardi worked day and night to raise money to pay for their return to a homeland that time and distance had transformed into a sunny garden of Eden. Maria resumed part-time work in the kitchen of the Lorenttis' cafe to supplement her full-time management of the boarding house. And Luigi's newspaper ad offering his musical services at private parties produced nearly twice as much revenue as he had previously earned performing at the now defunct dance hall. Private social gatherings where homemade wine filled the partial beverage void created by Prohibition, became the order of the day, particularly among the Piemontesi, where cellar production of wine and grappa was a time-honored tradition. Speakeasies had not yet appeared to absorb the more affluent part of the displaced patrons of the male-only saloons closed down by Prohibition.

While nobody could foresee it at the time, saloons were never to return even after Prohibition was repealed 14 years later by the 21st Amendment. Good riddance, in the view of Maria Suardi and many other politically conscious citizens of Spring Valley, who saw these oases as socially devastating, particularly in their effect on family life. Owned and operated by the same "captains of industry" who owned the mines, saloons attracted their working class patrons with cheap beer and free sandwiches and were packed to overflowing on Fridays. In the darkened street, women stood waiting. Some of them could be seen jumping up and down in an effort to catch the eye of a missing husband over the red velvet cafe curtain stretched across the front window to safeguard his privacy. Other women were at home with their children, waiting for what might be left of the family "breadwinner's" pay envelope.

Just seven years after passing through Ellis Island, Maria walked up the gangplank of the M.S. Colombo together with her husband and their daughter full of hope for a happy return to the Old Country. Maria was also getting full of her second baby, whose birth she reckoned to be at least two months away. After a week at sea, however, the unexpected happened and Maria was helped to the ship's hospital by her husband and a B Deck steward. Following a blessedly short period of labor, Maria gave premature birth to a son weighing in at a tiny 1,136 grams, just two and a half pounds.

Overjoyed by the birth of his son, Luigi ran out onto the deck to shout the good news to anyone who would listen. He then retrieved his accordion and played for anyone who would share his happiness. Dr. Riccardi, who delivered the baby had decidedly mixed feelings: he secretly wished that he had fathered the infant, and his happiness over the birth that he shared with Maria was cut short by his recognition of a painful professional duty he must perform. He sent for Luigi.

"My warmest congratulations to both of you dear people on the birth of your son," he said with a forced smile.

"Unfortunately," he said, and wished there were a better word to preface what he had to say, "I'm terribly sorry," which was even worse, he thought. "I regret that the small size of your baby does not give promise of a healthy life." Maria instinctively brought the swaddled buddle of new life as close as possible to her breast.

"He must live," she whispered, "my dear Doctor Riccardi, make him live."

"You know that I will do everything possible. I've already given instructions to my assistant to construct a cradle warmed by electricity – an incubator – such as those used in the large hospitals." He took a deep breath. "Still ..."

"Still?" asked Maria with pain creasing her face.

"Still, I think it would be advisable for you to have the ship's Chaplain, an ordained priest, christen your son as soon as possible."

Within minutes, Paul Suardi was received into the Catholic Church, and a few moments later the chaplain performed the rites to prepare him for leaving this world. And all the while, Maria squeezed the beads that her mother had given her and whispered the Rosary over and over until sleep overcame her. At that very instant, she smiled. It was a smile of pure contentment that appears only on the face of a mother holding her new life.

❖❖❖

In Torino, capital of the northern province of Piedmont at the base of the Alps, birthplace of the fertile lands of the Po River Valley, the marriage of Luigi and Maria Suardi reached a plateau, where it floundered. The marital union seemed to thrive on the incongruity of the area: a setting of natural beauty and tranquility suffused with the excitement of a muscular industrial giant intoxicated by political conflict. The couple knew that the intensity and spontaneity of their sex life had declined in this new environment. But they liked to believe that this change was part of the natural order of things and that, in any case, the fabric of their marriage was now strengthened by the bonds of love, obligation and duty weaved on the loom of their relationship with their two children.

The unravelling process, which first began outside the conscious perception of the principals, gained momentum and finally became irreversible in the latter stages of their three years (1919-1922) in Luigi's hometown.

Torino was, indeed, Luigi's town. He knew every street, the location of every marketplace, every shop, every restaurant, every barber shop, every bus stop and taxi stand. He knew the erratic schedules of trains and buses, where to buy tobacco for his pipe and tickets for the weekend soccer match. Maria had to ask her husband for directions to all of these places, and when she had to ask a second time, her generally patient husband answered in a mildly scornful tone. "But my dear Maria, I told you only yesterday ..." or, worse, "for the fourth time, the bus to the central market is number 33, which you catch at ..." The verbal irritations accumulated like flies on uncovered cheese.

Luigi was in his element playing for appreciative audiences (and huge tips) in a local trattoria. No longer would it be necessary to scrounge for money to put bread on the table by performing once or twice a week at private parties, where the guests, all strangers, seldom tipped. Moreover, there was no danger of a police raid to break up a good party in Torino. Here the wine flowed freely and Luigi never had to pay for his own glass. As time went on, Luigi's evening performances at the upscale French restaurant *Les Trois Garcons* grew into the morning hours, and his sleepy bedroom performances at home became less and less frequent, almost routine and finally almost a chore for both parties.

Maria was equally exhausted at the end of her day. In her preteens, Rosa was becoming increasingly independent and, it was clear to her mother, in greater need of being brought up within the bounds of a structured life based on solid Christian values. There were difficult questions Rosa put to her mother about life, religion and sexuality that now had to be answered, rules that suddenly needed to be explained rather than simply authorized by parental fiat.

The first years of her son's life were at least equally demanding of Maria's time and attention, and Paul's increasing need for physical space made Maria aware that the family would sooner rather than later have to secure a larger apartment. More importantly, Maria became convinced that she needed a better and safer neighborhood for her children. For centuries, Torino had been a city full of political fervor and national rivalries and had served as the first capital of the Kingdom of Italy. In the early 1920's, political differences moved onto a larger stage in northern Italy with the rapid growth of an expanding and suddenly unfranchised industrial working class, whose support was sought by both ends of the political spectrum. Driven by the success of the Bolshevik revolution in Russia, Italian revolutionaries split from the Italian Socialist Party to set up the Communist Party of Italy. At the same time, in Milano, Benito Mussolini created the totalitarian Fascist movement based on nationalist appeals to counter the threat posed by *Bolshevism*.

Maria's political sensibilities had been aroused by her experience with the miners, including violence-prone "Wobblies," in Spring Valley. She now saw equally ominous political forces at work. One morning as she shook the crumbs from a tablecloth out her fourth floor window, she heard shouts from the end of the street where she saw a group of young men wearing black shirts throwing bricks through the window of a Jewish shopkeeper. She caught sight of the man as he was dragged into the street and beaten by the bullies before they were driven off by the screams and curses hurled from windows up and down the street. Maria backed into her kitchen, sat down, and saw in a flashback as clear as light, as painful as a fist to the head, the bullies beating up Luigi in Spring Valley. As she sat sobbing, trying to clear her mind of the horrible sight, the strident sounds of a march sung incongruously by the high-pitched voices of young boys arose from the street. She looked out to see school children of the Fascist Youth organization wearing blue scarves and singing *Giovinezza*, a march composed for Mussolini's para-military Black Shirts organizations. Suddenly Paul appeared at the door and asked who was singing in the street.

"Nobody of any importance," said Maria, who then closed the window and distracted her son by steering him to the always-filled cookie jar. A few days later, Maria overheard her son humming the tune to *Giovinezza* and she made a decision: she must get Rosa and Paul away from Torino.

With Luigi's reluctant blessings, Maria left the next day with both of their children to visit her mother in Valperga. Much to her disappointment, Maria found that even the rural village had changed. Red flags flew from some balconies, Fascist flags from others. Slogans in red calling for the workers of the world to unite were painted over the next night with Fascist slogans calling for national strength and unity, and death to the Bolsheviks.

As much as Giovanna Boggio Roscio enjoyed the company of her daughter and grandchildren, she realized the dangers to all of them if they were to remain in Italy. After a late evening discussion in her garden, Giovanna stood up, wiped tears appearing in the corners of her eyes and told her daughter that she must leave the country. "For the good of your children, you must leave, my beautiful Maria." Her daughter nodded and went to bed. The next morning, Giovanna laid out her Tarot cards, which validated her daughter's decision to leave Italy, but warned of problems in her marriage. "Do you really believe what these cards say?" asked Maria. "I do, and you will, too," answered her mother, who then put the cards in a small box and presented them as a sort of farewell gift for a loving daughter whom she knew she would never see again in this life.

Maria embraced Giovanna, saw the sadness in her mother's eyes, whispered *arrivederci* and left for Torino.

When Maria reached home with her sleepy children, Luigi had already left for work. Maria felt relieved that she would get a night's sleep before telling her husband of her determination to return to the U.S. As she lay in bed waiting for sleep to overcome her anxiety, Maria rehearsed the arguments she intended to advance in support of her decision, but however compelling the reasons seemed to her, she was always left with a sinking feeling that mere words would never persuade Luigi to understand the wisdom of her determination to leave Italy. Her feelings, as usual, were accurate in forecasting his opposition.

"So what's so bad about this Mussolini character?" asked Luigi as the couple sat at the kitchen table drinking coffee. "And since when did you and your mama become such profound observers of the political situation in our country?" Although Maria was both hurt and offended with the way her husband's words were delivered in a tone edged with hostility she had never before heard, she remained politely silent in hopes that his anger would break up on the shoals of common sense. "The people I talk with, including some high ranking officials in the government – even the army and police – they tell me that we, our country, needs a strong leader if we're to put down the Bolsheviks and anarchists. Why, just a couple of years ago, these communists occupied the factories where they worked, right here in Torino. Don't you remember that?"

"Yes, I remember."

"Well, is that what you want? A bloody revolution like they got in Russia?" Luigi paused to catch his breath and poured himself another cup of coffee, confident that his irrefutable reasoning had put an end to the silly plan his wife had cooked up with her mother. "Think of the children, for God's sake!"

"The children, yes. They are uppermost in my thoughts, I can assure you," said Maria in a level voice that cut through the mounting tension like a scalpel. "I will not have our children dressed like toy soldiers marching through the streets singing the praises of an overstuffed braggart who struts around calling himself 'Il Duce.' And I will not permit our children to associate with bully boys wearing black shirts who go around beating up good people, like our grocer, just because they're Jews." Maria paused to catch her breath, and

Luigi thought it best not to challenge her arguments. He had never heard her speak in this way and was surprised by her knowledge of current events.

"My dear Maria," he said as he held up his hand like a schoolboy, "I know you want the best for our children. So do I. We just have a different view of what is best for them. I think that we are moving into a new and bright future here in Italy. I don't see Mussolini as a savior, but I think he is what our country needs, what we need."

Maria realized that she and Luigi stood at a crossroads and were about to take separate paths into the future. She kept her silence.

"Let's consider our situation from the practical point of view, my good wife. I am making good money here, at least twice as much as I ever earned in America. My tips alone bring in more money than my wages over there. Why, I ask you, should we move and in effect kill the goose who is laying the golden eggs for us here in Torino? Why, when my savings will make it possible for us to have a better home and better conditions for the children."

"Luigi, how long do you think it will take for you to save enough for us to enjoy a respectable standard of living?"

"I don't know. Maybe a year, maybe even less." Luigi took a deep breath and sighed in relief. "Then you agree to stay here in Torino?"

"No. We must leave here and go back to America. I will reopen my boarding house and in a year when you have collected enough golden eggs, you will join us."

Luigi Suardi remained silent as he considered Maria's plan. He experienced a rush of excitement, secretly nourishing the prospect of spending a year free of marital responsibilities and constraints.

Luigi got up, bent down to embrace his wife tenderly and whispered into her ear: "I shall miss you, my love.

But I must agree that your plan is best for the future of our whole family." Maria rose from her chair and kissed Luigi's ear, then moved to his mouth and licked his lips teasingly. She turned slightly sidewards and moved her hand down to feel him getting hard against her thigh.

"The children ...?"

"Are in the playground," whispered Maria as she unbuttoned his fly and led him – while maintaining her firm yet gentle grip – into the bedroom.

After completing a month's worth of lovemaking in the next few minutes, Maria and her husband lay still. "When do you plan ..."

"As soon as I can get Paul on our passport and book passage, my dear Luigi. Okay?"

Luigi then reached over to the chest of drawers that doubled as a nightstand and picked up the large hair-brush he had given his wife on her thirtieth birthday. The gift had brought her to tears when, and every time he brushed her soft and thick hair with it, she hummed a tune or simply, as now, purred like a kitten.

CHAPTER 12

As she went about preparing for her trip back to America, Maria experienced a new and different kind of happiness that lifted her in mind and body all day every day. It was a mood that danced through her veins, nestled in her head, and made her smile all the time, even to strangers passing on the street, to the priest hearing her confession at church, to the officials at the passport office who were used to being verbally abused by citizens forced to pay a bribe in addition to the standard fee to get their travel documents delivered in a reasonable time. Maria neither knew nor sought to know why she felt the way she did. It would be reasonable to attribute her uplifting *joie de vivre* to the expected support given her approaching adventure by her children, enhanced by the unexpected support tendered by her mother and husband. But her elation seemed to go beyond the limits of conscious reason. Maria felt, without questioning the feeling, that her elevated mood was in some way connected to her God-given power to see events that had happened, were happening or would take place in the future outside her immediate sensory field in time and space.

Although she failed to understand why it was that she always felt stimulated by major changes in her life, especially when these changes involved travel, Maria knew and enjoyed a sort of reciprocal effect that her mood produced in others. On her visit to the office of the steamship company in Genova to book passage to New York, Maria somehow realized that the clerk was being less than truthful when he advised her that unfortunately there was space left only in First Class for the October 28th sailing. She smiled, looked down at her children standing beside her, looked back at the man behind the counter and giggled. "Excuse me, sir" she said in a lowered voice through her white lace glove while she kept her cheerful eyes glued on his uniform jacket, "but I lack funds to travel in First Class, and I really must get on your ship on October twenty-eighth. And," she continued, her eyes now locked on his steel-rimmed spectacles, "*A l 'e' stuna' me na cioca ruta*," which meant that the man's assertions were out of tune like a cracked bell. The clerk excused himself and ducked into his supervisor's office.

"Chief, we've got a problem out there!"

"*Dio faus, stupido*, do you have to bring every little problem to me? Can't you see I have more important things to handle?"

"But Chief, I think this lady is something more than just one of your run-of-the-mill passengers. I sort of think that she may be sent by them," said the clerk pointing at the ceiling. "Maybe they suspect that we're selling some of the second class cabins at a, uh, premium and then ..." His superior frowned and the clerk continued, "You know, without letting *them* in on it."

"Hmm, that's no good. The officer stood up and took a long look at Maria through the two-way mirror mounted on the wall beside his desk. "What did you tell her?"

"I just said that there were no more Second Class cabins available, and didn't say anything about, you know, being able to get one for a little extra."

"Hmm. That's good. Now, let's not take any chances. Wait here for a couple of minutes and then go back and tell her that you were able to locate cabin space that had been reserved but you found it had just been cancelled. Got it?"

"Yes, boss. But what do you think she meant about being out of tune?"

"I don't know, but ..." he continued after taking a long second look through the mirror, "I do know that the woman at the counter is no ordinary second class passenger."

On October 28, 1922, Maria left on her second voyage to the U.S. During the same week, a man wearing a black suit and spats marched on Rome at the head of a column of Fascist militants wearing black shirts and jodhpurs. On the invitation of King Victor Emmanuel III, Benito Mussolini formed a new government. Like the power driven beneficiaries of social unrest elsewhere in Europe – Lenin in Russia and Hitler in Germany – Mussolini brought opponents of his party into the Cabinet. Few realized at the time that this gesture of national unity was no more than window dressing, even though the real focus of political power was openly revealed in a Fascist manifesto, which proclaimed: "From this moment, Mussolini *is* the government of Italy."

As the ship pulled away from the quay, a brass band of eight musicians in scraggly uniforms played the American and Italian national anthems, which caused both the travellers and their well wishers on shore to weep as they waved their handkerchiefs and shouted expressions of love and wishes for a safe journey. Maria held back her tears as she looked down at Luigi from the boat deck and kissed her lucky old coin, a smile of hope and promise playing at the corners of her mouth. She was determined to control her emotions, to hide any signs of sorrow from her children, and succeeded in this effort until the liner turned seaward and her beloved Luigi slipped out of sight. It was then that the sounds of his accordion playing *Maria, Mari* reached her ears through the discordant sounds of the band mingled with the squawking of the ever-hungry sea gulls escorting the Colombo. Suddenly all of the confidence she had built up to buttress her decision to leave vanished, washed away in a deluge of tears. Carrying Paul in her arms, Maria struggled to reach her cabin when a tall man in the uniform of a ship's officer took her arm. "Oh, Doctor Riccardi. Thank God, oh, thank God. You're always here when I need ..." Maria fell into the strong arms of the man who helped her to her cabin and put her and the children to bed for needed sleep.

Elated by his unexpected reunion with Maria, Dr. Riccardi moved quickly to arrange for an upgrade of her accommodations. Her assigned cabin in Second Class was a giant step above Steerage, but it was located in the middle of the ship where the lighting was dim, there was no porthole and Maria had to share her twin-sized bunk with Paul. Guido Riccardi embarked on his mission. First stop: the First Class purser, Gino Madalena.

"Ciao, Gino, have you got all the sheep herded into their stalls?"

"Si, Doctor, all but one, who unfortunately missed the boat. Probably hung over in some whorehouse in Torino."

"Are you going to go back for him?"

"Never. Late for a ship sailing is no problem at all for this old geezer. He could buy the Colombo with the change he carries around to tip bellhops!"

"And First Class pursers?"

"Yes, Guido. And that gives me one big pain, right where I live," said the purser patting the wallet in his back pocket. "Why does this always have to happen to me?"

"Wait, Gino, I think I see a silver lining in the cloud hanging over you at this moment," said the ship's doctor as he raised his hand and looked at the clock above and behind the purser's head that was just chiming eight times for 4 o'clock in the afternoon. "And I can hear it all well." The purser's look of nauseated skepticism failed to dim Riccardi's enthusiasm. "Come with me for two minutes. I have a bottle of Pernod in my cabin that will, I assure you, clear your head and enable you to see the silver lining for yourself." With a shrug and a signal for his assistant to take over, Gino followed Riccardi a few steps down the passageway to his cabin. The doctor unlocked the cabinet over his desk and extracted a bottle of Pernod. He then carefully measured ten cubic centiliters of the clear yellow liquid into a chemist's beaker and then added distilled water to bring the suddenly clouded aperitif to the half liter line. He then poured equal portions of the anise-flavored liqueur into two highball glasses and proposed a toast.

"To the poor bastard who missed the boat, and in doing so provided a cabin for my poor niece and her two children. And" Riccardi continued, raising his glass a second time to forestall the questions forming on the lips of the purser, "to a most gracious Purser, whose compassion will be rewarded both in heaven and," the doctor discreetly slipped a handful of lira notes into the Purser's hand, "right down here on the high seas."

"Thank you, Dr. Riccardi," said the purser, Gino Madalena, as he slowly moved the Pernod around his teeth before swallowing it. He then carefully put down the glass and raised the banknotes to count them. "Isn't it ironic," he mused, "that the value of a currency is always inversely proportionate to its artistic quality?"

"How's that?"

"Well, just look at this note: the paper on which it is printed is like the finest silk, yet," the purser pulled at both ends of the bill, "it is as strong as leather. And perceive the watermark – a perfectly detailed image of Michelangelo's 'David' as if you were standing before the statue itself. And the colors! Not a single dominant pigment such as those vulgar American 'greenbacks.' No, we have here a softly nuanced tones every color of the rainbow." He raised a bill to his lips, and kissed it and smiled with all of his teeth showing.

"Yes, yes, I certainly agree," said the ship's doctor, as he looked down and moved his glass about in both hands to cover his embarrassment.

"And yet, the exquisite aesthetics of our currency only serve to conceal its paltry value. Beautiful," he said as he wadded the bills together and stuffed them into his pants pocket, "and not worth the paper they're printed on!"

"Perhaps I gave you too ..."

"Not at all, you are most generous, Doctor. The only problem is that there are other employees of our beloved shipping lines, all of whom, I'm sure you realize, are rather shamelessly underpaid and have to humiliate themselves before their filthy rich first class masters in hopes of getting a decent gratuity for their services." Counting on his fingers, the purser continued. "First, there is the dining room steward and his staff, including the chef, the wine steward and the waiters." Madalena paused. "I'm assuming, I hope correctly, that your, uh, niece and her children may not be in a position to tip as generously as most of the passengers in First Class."

Dr. Riccardi nodded his assent as he took out his billfold from his jacket pocket.

"Then we have the cabin personnel ..."

"Yes, yes, I quite understand, Do you suppose that this will be enough to satisfy the needs of all of these worthies?" he asked as he placed a sheaf of notes in the purser's outstretched hand.

Counting the bills by bending down their corners with the practiced thumb of a bank teller, the purser smiled. "Yes, my dear doctor, I'm sure that this will be quite sufficient. And now, if you will be good enough to write down the name of your niece, if you don't mind, that is – any name will do – so that I can make the necessary entry in the First Class passenger manifest, et cetera. You understand there is much to be done."

"I understand, Signor Madalena," said Dr. Riccardi, as a queasy feeling crept up inside him and made him seek some distance from the man who suddenly and inexplicably made him feel so thoroughly uncomfortable. The purser felt the coolness and with a look at his watch and a remark about having a whole lot of work to do, emptied his glass and left, Doctor Riccardi alone to nurse his misery. Why did that son of a bitch make me feel this way, so dirty? After all, the purser agreed to do exactly what I wanted him to do. He's arranging to have my beloved Maria moved into a fine cabin on the Promenade Deck, where the children will have a double bunk in their own separate bedroom, and that way Maria will have her own room and ... yes, that's what I wanted, didn't I? Her own bedroom, where I can bring her after we have stood on deck hugging and kissing, deeply, picking up where we left off – when was it: eight, nine, a hundred years ago? – moving as one, naturally synchronized with the gentle roll and pitch of the ship, in tune with the rhythmical throbbing of its engines, gaining a measure of warmth against the chilly winds gusting off above the swirling waters of the North Atlantic, where we can then come in and quickly, quietly get undressed and into the large bed, where Maria will open her body and soul to bring me into her, will rise to enfold my deep presence, where we will fulfill our love as it is destined to be fulfilled.

"Oh, Maria," he groaned as his fantasy surged and released in a warm flood, creating yet another layer of shame. Which worsened the guilt and self-hate that had come to envelope and overwhelm Doctor Guido Riccardi, and remained with him as a constant companion during the remainder of the weeklong voyage. Guido and Maria met on several occasions, including dinner each evening at the table of the ship's Captain, who was enraptured by the unspoiled beauty of the doctor's "niece," whose phony kinship with one of his officers made her seem somehow accessible. Even, perhaps to the ship's master, he mused, and spent every dinner playing up to her and to her children, whom anyone could see held the key to her heart.

Maria pretended to be unaware of the family relationship alleged to exist between Riccardi and her, and it was never mentioned, because no one believed it to be true and, therefore, everyone sought to avoid possible embarrassment which might be caused by alluding to it. Of course, all of the good doctor's fellow officers, including the captain, assumed Maria to be his mistress, which assumption was expressed in ill-concealed winks and smirks. And these signals, when intercepted by Riccardi, served to exacerbate his feelings of guilt for what he had done and shame for having demeaned this woman for whom he had the highest regard.

Maria, for her part, made the most of a good thing. The elegant cabin, the haute cuisine served at the captain's table, the cabin attendants who doubled as babysitters for her children every evening, the deck chairs into which the family members were wrapped by deck stewards, all of these amenities were enjoyed to the fullest as simply the good fortune, which Maria told her children, always befalls those who mind their manners and live according to the rules laid down by the Church and enforced by their parents.

Of course, Maria had no illusions about her doctor friend's motives in providing these amenities. In the nearly nine years that had passed since their first encounter, Dr. Riccardi had aged. He had put on weight, especially in his face, where his once sharply sculpted features were now encased in fleshy outcroppings, which made his mouth and grey eyes seem smaller. Most people would still call him handsome, but the visible physical changes in Dr. Riccardi struck Maria as signs of some sort of inner decay. It was as if he had plastered over the hurt he had suffered earlier in life with short-lived satisfactions and a layer of cynical scar tissue. Maria knew within minutes after their reunion that the life – indeed the very soul – of this man for whom she had felt love had been permanently changed; its pure wellsprings of unconditional love irreversibly contaminated.

After dinner on the last night out, as the Colombo steamed slowly through the kelp-scented fog shrouding the coast of New England, Maria took Riccardi's hand and led him onto the dance floor. As dancers crowded the floor to show off their dancing school skills, the couple became screened from the envious stares of diners seated at the captain's table, and Maria whispered to Guido to follow her.

They climbed a ladder to the boat deck, where Maria backed her Guido up against the railing, pulled his head down and kissed him flush on the mouth. "Thank you, Uncle Guido."

"Wh, what ...," said Dr. Riccardi, who then looked down into Maria's upturned face with its innocently wide-spaced eyes sparkling over a sensuously full mouth that smiled up at him from a resolute jaw, and chuckled. Maria chuckled back and in seconds they joined in a wonderfully uninhibited, emotionally cleansing howl of laughter.

"Seriously, now ..." said Maria and triggered another round of laughter, which only subsided after both parties held their sides in happy pain. "I do want to thank you for making this voyage a joy that my children and I will cherish for the rest of our lives. And please," she added, raising her hand to set a limit to Guido's attempted embrace, "let's not do anything that will complicate, or cheapen, this wonderful, truly magical experience."

"I love you, Maria."

"And I love you, too."

As the couple started back down the ladder, Maria stopped abruptly, and put her hand on Guido's shoulder.

"Wait, listen. Do you hear that?"

"No, I hear nothing except when our ship's horn sounds its fog signal."

"Wait," said Maria looking straight ahead into the fog. Now I can see it." It's a ship heading straight for us." Dr. Riccardi looked at Maria and could see even in the dim light that her eyes were tightly closed as she continued, "Guido, you must hurry to the bridge and warn them." The doctor hesitated, noting that Maria's eyes were still unopened, but sprinted to the bridge when her eyes suddenly opened and focused on his and her request became an order he could not ignore. "Go," she commanded.

And so it was that Maria's clairvoyant perception of a collision of two ships on the high seas, enabled the ship's doctor on the Colombo to alert the helmsman to change course over the disjointed objections of the First Officer, whose consumption of Chianti had dulled his senses. The doctor later received a medal for heroism.

Maria received a much higher reward: the survival of her son and daughter.

CHAPTER 13

The Lorenttis had told Maria before she left on her trip to Italy that she, Luigi and the children would always be welcome as family members in their large Victorian home if and when they should return to Spring Valley. So it was with genuine pleasure that the couple read the telegram from New York announcing Maria's return, although they were puzzled that the message made no mention whatever of Luigi.

"MY HELPERS ROSA AND PAUL WILL MAKE STUFFED ONIONS FOR DINNER NOVEMBER SECOND STOP LOVE MARIA."

The cryptic message told them all they needed to know: She would arrive on the Illinois Central train at 4:32 p.m. and would prepare their favorite dish for supper. Maria and her children would stay with them for an indefinite time, and the childless Alice and Grande were delighted with the prospect. After repeatedly consulting his Hamilton watch which rested in his lefthand vest pocket, Grande announced that they had better leave for the depot to meet their guests. It was not yet four o'clock and the trip to the depot never took more than five minutes, but Grande wanted to get to the station well before the train's arrival. It was a way to demonstrate his admiration for the railroads and everything they stood for: their powerful steam-spouting locomotives moving people and freight from sea to shining sea, moving on their broad shoulders the tangible wealth of what was fast becoming the most powerful country in the world. And doing the job on time, by God. So what if the senior Vanderbilt had scoffed "the public be damned." So what? Maybe the masses of little people with their petty self-interested concerns, and the socialists who appealed to them by promising them something for nothing, deserved to be damned for standing in the way of Progress. "And that's spelled with a capital "P," as he had told his fellow Rotarians at their luncheon only a week ago. Yes, Grande loved the railroads and what they stood for, just as he loved his heavy timepiece, like the ones used by railroad conductors, attached to one end of a gold chain with a small gold jack knife at the other end resting in his right-hand vest pocket. He even loved the soot-darkened red brick depot, with its freight wagons designed to be drawn by horses parked at exactly the spot where the baggage car would stop; the barred ticket window that only opened when the station master peeked out and saw a line of at least three would-be travellers lined up at it; the solid oak benches in the waiting room that were harder than church pews but still comfortable enough for use by the town drunk to sleep off his latest bout with liquor substitutes more devastating than the forbidden juice itself; and, the solid brass cuspidors that had never been emptied of their unsightly contents of water blackened with spit, tobacco juice and dis-

integrating cigar butts, nor purged of their pervasive and
pleasingly foul sweet-sour smell.

At 4:32, Grande extracted his watch, gently moved it
up and down to enjoy its heft, and frowned. "Why," he
wondered out loud for the benefit of Alice and the station master on the unlikely chance that he might be within earshot, "does the railroad always publish such pre-
cise times if they never intend to stick to them. I mean,
wouldn't a rounded off time be close enough, like, say,
4:30 or 4:45?" Alice smiled up at her big husband as he
tucked the Hamilton back into its warm pouch. She
knew that he singled out for criticism this one insignifi-
cant shortcoming of the Illinois Central only to highlight
by contrast the overall quality of the line's performance.
"Be right back," Grande said, as he buttoned his camel's
hair topcoat and in line with tradition, swung open the
massive door to move out onto the platform. After a
quick look at the red and green lights and forearms of the
semaphore signal a hundred yards to the east, he swung
back into the depot to announce "she's comin'."

Nervous expressions of how well everyone looked
and how much the children had grown were soon
drowned in a silent sea of love. The Lorenttis' *family* was
reunited at last. Soon, Maria's fatigue gave way to the
creative exhilaration she always felt in the kitchen. Eight
onions were boiled just long enough to be tender but not
mushy. Their centers were adroitly extracted and
ground, mixed with cinnamon, veal, grated Parmesan,
raisins, ground bread sticks, butter, cream and eggs, four
yokes and two whites, then returned to their "shells" to
be baked to a golden brown on top. *Voila*. Italian stuffed
onions! Eaten to an accompaniment of Grande's excellent red wine (Maria wondered how he had come across
the unlabeled bottles and made a mental note to ask him
about it) and Alice's equally excellent bread, it was a
meal fit for royalty. Afterwards the exhausted guests

retired, Maria and Rosa cuddled in the big walnut poster bed and Paul huddled on a canvas cot he loved because it made him feel like he was in the Army. They all said their prayers. Then, just before falling into the arms of Orpheus, as Maria used to say, Paul's tiny voice crept across the chilly bedroom:

"Mama."

"Yes, Paul, what is it?"

"When is Papa coming home?"

"Very soon, my boy, very soon," she answered as a swelling of doubt moved into her chest and teardrops forced their way into the corners of her closed eyes.

The family of three, lacking a sorely-missed husband and father for reasons that now seemed inadequate, even trivial, fell into a sleep that only long-haul truck drivers and combat infantrymen can experience, a rejuvenating state of sensory nullity in a time/space cocoon, insensible for twelve hours, an eternity.

A few days later, after Sunday Mass, Maria sent her children out to play in the wrought iron fenced yard and took Alice aside for a heart-to-heart. Over her hostesses' objections that the young family was more than welcome to stay through the winter, Maria insisted that she needed a home for her children, a place they could call their own, a place where their father could return to. "I hate to ask for more help from you and Grande," she said, "why, I'm not even sure how Ill ever be able to replay you for the kindness you've already shown me, and ..." Her lips were stilled by the hand of Alice, who smiled and whispered, "My dear child, I understand your need to get into a home of your own, for the children's sake above all, and it will be our pleasure to help you find this home. I'll just get Grande now, if you don't mind."

"No, of course I don't mind."

As Alice Lorentti reached the dining room doors, she turned and with an uncharacteristically stern look punctuated by a slightly raised left eyebrow, said in slow, measured words, "I warn you, Maria: you must never mention to Grande anything about repaying us for our help to you and your children. This would be a grave insult to him. Do you understand, my child?"

"Yes, my dear Alice," said Maria as she scurried across the room to take her benefactor's hand in both of hers, "I do understand. We are family and we are, after all ..."

"Italian."

"Oh, yes, Alice. We are Italian. The two embraced and shared a few tears.

❖❖❖

Maria was wearing a long black skirt and a primly starched white blouse peeking out from a fitted vest when she entered the office of the President of the Spring Valley branch of the Illinois State Bank, Aden O'Bern. O'Bern, who disdained changing his name from the original Gaelic spelling into the popular "O'Brien" used by many Irish-Americans, was one of the few remaining immigrants from the Auld Sod to hold a leading position in the community. Irishman Charles Devlin, who founded the city's first coal mining company and served as its first mayor, had built and lost a financial empire before moving to Kansas to make another fortune.Generally speaking, the Irish nourished ill feelings toward the *late-comer* Italian immigrants, whom they regarded as political radicals and Wobbly labor agitators not to be trusted. And the feeling was mutual, as Italians did little to disguise their contempt for the Irish whom they regarded as barroom brawlers not to be trusted. Of course, neither of these ethnic groups liked the Jewish inhabitants, both of them agreeing that the citizens of Hebraic persuasion were very simply not to be trusted.

"I'm pleased to meet you, Signora, uh ..."

"Mrs. Luigi Suardi," said Maria as she turned to let the bank president take her coat. As he did so, his twinkling blue eyes danced up and down over the curvature beneath the white blouse, accentuated by the constraining dark green velvet bodice.

"Ah, yes, indeed, Mrs. Suardi. By the way, I don't see your husband. Is he unable to join us today? Indisposed?"

"No, you see, he is in Italy, and is not expected to return here for several months, uh, weeks."

"That's a great pity. I'm sure it must make life difficult for you, being here alone with your children."

"Oh, we make out as best we can. But it would be quite helpful if we could borrow, say $500 to buy a small bungalow that Mr. Lorentti has located on 7th Street."

"Well, yes, I'm quite sure that would make your life easier, and I only hope that I shall be able to secure an adequate mortgage loan for you," said the bank president as he hung up Maria's coat and quickly closed his office door with its snowflake half window concealing the lobby and the two tellers working there from view.

"Now, don't you worry your pretty head," he said as he moved behind Maria and patted her hair, and when she showed no resistance to this gesture, moved his hands to her shoulders and then downwards, slowly sliding them to the inside until he index fingers made contact softly with her protruding breasts whose rising and falling he took to signal sensual arousal on her part. He was convinced that she would most certainly be his before the mortgage papers were signed.

Turning away from Maria, O'Bern cleared his throat, took a deep breath, quickly walked around his desk and seated himself in his high-backed leather and rosewood throne. Seemingly absorbed in the papers in front of him, he said, "You realize, Mrs. Suardi, that it is highly unusual, in fact it has never happened in this bank, that a mort-gage loan would ever be granted to a woman."

"I understand," said Maria in a low voice that beto-kened total submission to the man seated across the desk from her. "But I do so hope that somehow some kind of arrangement can be reached," she added, slowly raising her head and locking her wide-set eyes onto his eager eyes, as a slight smile moved her full lips.

"Yes, uh, I'm quite sure it can," said the educated son of an uneducated foreman at Mine #1. So, if you will kindly fill out these papers at home and return them, let's say, at the close of business, five o'clock, say, this afternoon, we can get your application moving. Just come around to the back entrance here and, ha, ha, knock twice on this door. Then after we finish our little busi-ness, perhaps you would do me the honor of joining me in a little celebration right here in my office. You see, I managed to set aside a private supply right here," he said, opening a cabinet door behind his desk to reveal a well-stocked bar.

"I'd be delighted," said Maria evenly, with her eyes focused at a point just below the tip of her interlocutor's large nose. If they'd never had that potato famine, we'd be running the banks and the police force, too, she thought as she took the mortgage application papers in one hand and gracefully offered her other hand to be kissed by this hot little leprechaun.

At ten minutes past five that afternoon, Aden O'Bern answered the knock at the rear of his office. He had painstakingly set the stage for what the blood racing to his forehead announced as the relief that would soon come from his humdrum existence at home with a hag-gard, nagging and prematurely graying wife and their seven children. Only half of the new incandescent lights were turned on, fresh orange blossom potpourri sweet-ened the musty air in the office, and the newspapers that had desecrated the fine oxblood leather sofa were gone, replaced with a large satin-covered pillow.

The anticipated double knock on the door, rather too loud for the hand of a little woman, resounded through the office and startled O'Bern. Perhaps she had struck the door with her umbrella handle, he thought, as he moved to the door while adjusting his cravat.

Good evening, Mr. O'Bern."

"Why, good evening Mr. Lorentti. Won't you come in."

Grande entered the office, looked around to take in the redecoration obviously designed in preparations for a tryst and returned his penetrating gaze straight into and through the eyes of the bank president, who nervously offered his surprise visitor a chair. Grande remained silent as he removed his topcoat, threw it on the sofa and took a seat beside the desk, his coal black eyes riveted on his reluctant host.

"To what do I owe the pleasure of this unexpected visit, Mr. Lorentti?"

"The pleasure is all mine, Mr. O'Bern. I am here to conclude the business Mrs. Suardi initiated this morning."

"Oh, you know Mrs. Suardi?"

"Why, yes, Mrs. Lorentti and I think of her as our daughter. As a matter of fact, she and her children are at the moment guests in our home, awaiting the return of Mr. Suardi from Italy."

"That's nice. And what can I do for you."

"You can authorize the issuance of a mortgage loan in the amount of $500 to Mrs. Suardi for the purchase of a four room house at 38 Seventh Street. I believe you will find these papers to be in perfect order."

"Yes, I'm sure, but you see the bank has to follow certain guidelines and, uh, rules, Mr. Lorentti. And as much as I would personally like to see Mrs. Suardi get the funds to purchase the house on Seventh Street, I'm afraid that the bank does not permit giving a mortgage to a woman."

"That is not my understanding of what you told Mrs. Suardi when she visited you earlier today."

"Well, no, uh, that's quite right. I suppose I did give her the impression that she could get the loan, but ..."

"Then I suppose you are a man of your word." O'Bern nodded his assent. "And I further suppose that you will sign on this line, Mr. O'Bern, authorizing the issuance of the loan."

"Yes, of course," said the bank president, who hurriedly signed the application before making a last ditch effort at regaining a measure of self-respect. "I trust that Mr. Lorentti will be willing to guarantee mortgage payments by signing as a co-maker?"

"No. You have my word that I guarantee Mrs. Suardi's repayment of the loan. That is all you need, and that is all you will get."

Maria got her little bungalow and Aden O'Bern never again made the mistake of mixing business with pleasure, either of the real or merely anticipated variety.

CHAPTER 14

Luigi Suardi left *Les Trois Garcons* because the three brothers who owned the place could never agree on anything – prices, menu, music – except the indisputable fact that anything French was far superior to anything Italian. Often the proprietors even spoke in French, a language with which Luigi had only a passing acquaintance, thus rudely placing him outside the decision-making process. This was particular irksome to a professional entertainer who knew that his music was at least as important as the Provencal cuisine featured by the brothers in attracting and holding their customers. At times, the owners would add insult to injury by insisting that Luigi include in his repertoire French songs that were unknown to him and most of the restaurant's clientele.

Before walking out of the place, however, Luigi took care to line up employment at *Mangia*, a somewhat smaller trattoria a few blocks away that proudly featured the kind of romantic Italian ballads that Luigi played and sang so well. He took a cut in pay but this was more than compensated by his being able to rent at nominal cost a nicely appointed apartment with an adjoining roofed patio on the top floor immediately above the restaurant. After his first night of playing for an appreciative audience dominated by members of the Fascisti elite, Luigi walked out on his patio, inhaled deeply of the sweet evening air, stroked the leaves of the potted palm, gazed at the full moon that illuminated the scene and its companion evening star that would soon be renamed the morning star, and felt at one with God and His world. Luigi sank to his knees on the cold tile floor and cried. Through his tears, Luigi Suardi whispered aloud into his folded hands, "Maria, God bless you and keep you, and please God bring us together again." After a long pause, Luigi took a deep breath and begged out loud for his beloved to forgive him for letting her to go America.

Luigi Suardi would soon have another and graver reason to seek forgiveness.

Francesca Bernardin was attracted to Luigi Suardi by his music, which produced in her feelings of such sensual awareness that, like a narcotic, she was irresistibly drawn to his stage to avoid physical illness. She had twice tried to stay away from *Mangia*, but on each occasion felt such severe discomfort that she was forced to return to the place to see the musician with the black, dancing eyes and the long, sweeping black mustache, and to hear the soft, smoothly sculpted passages that he coaxed from the black leather instrument that he held so securely in hands both strong and tender. Francesca had given sizeable gratuities to the head waiter, which provided her with sole possession of a leather upholstered chair at a tiny round table in a dark corner of the lounge between the anteroom, where guests sipped their Campari and soda while awaiting the arrival of their partners, and the spacious dining room that extended away from the street to double glass doors that in fair weather opened onto a terrace bedecked with plants in ornate terra-cotta pots and vines festooned from over-head trellises. Positioned at a discreet angle behind him, francesca was able to watch the musician's every move without revealing her increasingly obsessive interest either to him or to any of the diners. As could be expected, it often happened that single males noticed and tried to strike up an acquaintance with this beautiful blonde woman with the large blue eyes sitting alone in the bar. It was usually enough for the woman, who was obviously a person of class and good breeding, to dismiss these approaches by reference to a husband who would soon join her. This polite deterrent was sometimes documented with a second glass on her table half-filled with wine from the Asti Spumante bottle resting in the ice bucket. If the uninvited guest persisted in his efforts to share her company, Francesca simply raised her glass, which was a signal to the ever-vigilant maitre d' to intervene in her behalf and politely remove the intruder. In the rare instances when the intruder returned to force himself on her, this fine lady got rid of him by expressing an out-of-character vulgarity such as *"Va a cagate dos!"* (go shit on yourself) or, simply, *"tirte su la cerniera ad le braie"* (pull up your zipper), which invariably caused the interloper to look down with an expression of embarrassment and then up with an expression of utter stupidity.

During Francesca's second appearance at *Mangia,* Luigi acknowledged her presence as he concluded a break with a glass of wine bought for him by another customer in the bar. "To your health," he mouthed as he raised his glass in her direction. "And to yours," she responded in a resonant contralto voice that rode its low frequency pitch across the room and straight into his viscera. This brief exchange made the woman's presence more than a temporary distraction; during the following two nights, both his playing and his singing suffered to the extent that the owner noticed and asked if Luigi were ill. The truth was that this woman had intruded into the depths of his soul, thereby causing the musician to lose his power to concentrate on his music, or anything other than her presence. When the restaurant was closing up on the third night, Luigi hurriedly secured his accordion and confronted Francesca at her table. "Excuse me, but what are you doing here?" he asked. When she answered only with a tiny smile, he continued in a polite but deeply troubled voice, "Who are you. Why are you here?"

"I am Francesca Bernardin," she replied slowly. "And I think you know why I am here."

"Yes, well, I live right upstairs. Would you do me the honor ..."

"Yes, Signor Suardi, I'd be delighted."

Luigi didn't hear her on the stairs, but as he fumbled for his door key, her abdomen touched his backside and stayed there while her mouth moved up to the base of his neck. Her breath was hot and came in shortened intervals.

Dear God, he thought, if I don't get away from her now ... And he turned around to face her, to speak to her, which brought first their eyes and then their mouths together. She slid one hand down to greet his aroused organ and with the other hand turned the key to open the door behind him. She led him straight to the bed while disrobing on the way, leaving her dress and slight undergarments in a trail on the floor. She slid half way under the comforter and urged him with her upheld arms to hurry getting out of his cloths. Luigi realized he had no time to think, no time or inclination to weigh the consequences of what, with certain inevitability, was in process. He took her large breast in his hand and with pent up sexual desire licked its hard nipple, then sucked, but the dampness between her spread legs signalled that any further foreplay would be redundant, that she craved to have his swollen penis enter her, drive into her, through her into total release, to dominate by being dominated by this man, her lover.

Luigi had heard men speak of women like this, hot-breathing females whose sexual appetites were insatiable. One friend had finally had to leave his nymphomaniacal mistress because of physical exhaustion that left him unable to work. Every afternoon when he returned home, she greeted him at the door to their apartment wearing a full length rabbit fur with nothing underneath. He was denied even a few minutes to relax with a glass of wine before she laid him on the divan beside the entry door or on top of the fur coat dropped on the vestibule floor. Unable to maintain the pace of this enforced sex life, but unwilling to decelerate at the risk of losing his self respect as a redblooded Italian male, Luigi's musician friend had moved south to Tuscany where he met and married a woman whose work in the vineyards imposed acceptable limits on her conjugal demands.

For three nights, Francesca followed Luigi to his room and consumed him, making love on the sofa, in bed and on the breakfast table until, on the fourth night, as he lay fast asleep, she got up and dressed, took a pair of scissors and snipped off the ends of his waxed mustache, placed them underneath the pillow beside him, and left, never to return. Luigi was surprised to find the bed empty beside him in the morning and shocked to discover when he prepared to shave that the grand extensions on the mustache it had taken him years to cultivate were missing. *Troia*, he muttered, followed by *vaca*, another Piemontesi expression for a whore, before he took his razor and removed what was left under his nose. He could explain his decision to get rid of the whole thing (the clean-shaven Mussolini had inspired many Italians associated with the new ruling class to follow his example) but Luigi would never be able to explain to others the actual circumstances of losing the best parts of his mustache. It was even more difficult to rid himself of the ugly residue of shame that the beautiful Francesca had left behind to numb his conscience. It became increasingly difficult for him to write his wife. Instead of the genuine expressions of love that had permeated his letters and had flowed effortlessly from his pen, his letters were now filled with the prosaic details of his life with salutations of love stiffly, almost formally, worked in to serve as necessary packaging. Try as he night to rid himself of her, Francesca kept jumping into his mind's eye, even after he was told by a friend that soon after her disappearance from *Mangia* she had appeared at a club frequented by members of the Torino AC soccer team. According to his informant, Francesca had presented the innkeeper at *Strikers* bar with a list of the Torino players on whim she wished to bestow her luscious favors. At last report she had bedded five members of the Italian League championship team, including its famous striker, two midfielders and the goalkeeper.

Unable to purge the woman Francesca from his mind, Luigi was thankfully rescued from his torment by the simple process of substitution. Karla Leone, daughter-in-law of the owner of *Mangia,* was an olive-skinned brunette of ample proportions, who grew up in Sicily and wrote off the language spoken in the northern Italian provinces as an insoluble mystery. Not that she needed to expend must linguistical effort in carrying out her pasta preparations in the kitchen. Directions to the kitchen staff consisted of screams and curses directed at his assistants by the chef. The pitch and volume of his words was more important than their meaning, and

Karla understood his inflections as well as anyone. Still, she resented his insulting snarls, not least of all because he was a distant relative of her father-in-law who was her boss, and her husband, who tried to upgrade his image by acting like her boss. She would show them. She would get revenge and Luigi would be her chosen instrument for this purpose. This decision came to Karla when she saw Francesca slip up the stairs to Luigi's flat before closing time several weeks earlier. He was married to a woman in America, she had heard, but he was obviously fair game in Torino.

Before his performance Luigi always came into the kitchen and served himself a light supper. On the night Karla had chosen to make her move, Luigi was reaching into the ice box for some salami when Karla came up behind him, close enough for her perfumed presence to be sensed without physical contact. He turned and inadvertently touched her bosom, the fullness of which had dislodged a button at the top on her starched white shirt, the most sensually provocative garment a woman can wear. Luigi excused himself and Karla nodded her forgiveness and presented an earthenware bowl containing Alfredo sauce. "Taste it, please," she said. Since she offered no utensil, he held up an index finger. "So?" he asked and she nodded. "Ummm, excellente!" She took his hand, scooped up some more of the creamy sauce with his finger and took in into her mouth. She licked it, but kept his finger in her grasp as she looked Luigi straight in the eye, licked her lips with a nod and a smile, pronounced the sauce acceptable and then took another sampling from the bowl and this time stuck his whole finger into her mouth for a few seconds before sucking it as she pulled her head back. "When?" he asked. "Tonight," she responded. He pointed upwards. She nodded. He handed her the keys to his flat, and that was that. Even without a mustache, Luigi realized he was still irresistible.

Karla was as good as she had given him reason to hope. There was no conversation, only body language, intensely concentrated by Karla's need to return home in the unlikely case that her husband would be waiting for her. Luigi was especially delighted by what she did with her mouth and tongue. She was equally pleasured by his creative positioning, making use of his arm and upper body strength to turn her over on the floor. And then – how she loved this part – he would lift her legs up and around his hips while he stood up to use her as a wheelbarrow.

One night as the couple lay in bed engulfed in a peaceful cloud of sexual satisfaction, Karla asked in a matter-of-fact tone if Luigi were married. The question went unanswered, left suspended in air like a turd in a punchbowl, as Luigi slowly slipped out of bed and went to the bathroom, where his remorse bubbled to the surface in tearful convulsions. On his return, he poured a glass of wine from a carafe on the nightstand and emptied it in a single draft before returning into the arms of his lover. "I'm sorry," she whispered and gently cradled his genitalia, moved her head down to let both his love and his sadness grow into her.

Unlike the one-night stands with single women willing to share his need for short-term sexual gratification, Luigi's adulterous affair with karla continued for months on quite a different and higher level of consciousness. In some strange way that Luigi failed to understand, their relationship seemed mysteriously enriched and protected by the very fact that both of them were married. Rather than feeling doubly damned by not only committing the mortal sin of adultery but by doing it with a married woman, an adulteress in her own right, Luigi experienced a sense of liberation from moral guilt, feeling that his adultery was balanced by hers. And Karla experienced the same added pleasure in the subconscious satisfaction that his adultery negated the sin of her own act of marital infidelity. Especially since this was her first extramarital experience. It was also her last, because her husband found out about it and beat her to a pulp on he return home early one morning.

Luigi then suffered an extended term of celibacy to avoid a threatened beating by Karla's cuckholded mate. Then one day in the spring of 1925, Sophia, a recently widowed wife of a local green grocer twice her age appeared. In need of an income to supplement her meager widow's pension, she had polished her throaty vocalist talent and taken a job singing ballads to Luigi's accompaniment on Saturday nights. She first became romantically interested in the musician when she saw Karla sneaking up the stairs to his flat. When Karla failed to appear the following Saturday, Sophia pounced like a kitten. Feigning a headache at the close of their performance, she persuaded Luigi to give her an aspirin in his flat. He gave her the potion and more. An avid skier, Sophia's thighs had developed enormous strength, which stimulated Luigi's thrusts to depths that surprised both participants and left them wet and sore. Their Saturday night trysts went on for weeks until Sophia left *Mangia* and Suardi as suddenly as she had arrived, to his relief.

Then came Gina, a busty member of the Black Shirts auxiliary assigned to recruit Luigi into the local chapter of the Fascist party, which was rapidly consolidating its political power throughout Italy. He was an easy target once he joined her on the desk in the otherwise abandoned back room of the party headquarters. Later he wondered if his afternoon sessions involving both political and sexual indoctrination by this skilled Tyrolean practitioner were worth the party dues which took a sizeable chunk from his earnings, tips included.

His party dues and gifts to his friends and some time companions had defeated Luigi's periodic resolutions to save money for a triumphant return to Maria. At the same time, he was deriving diminished satisfaction from the more or less short-term gratifications of his carnal appetite. Luigi was forced to bite the bullet of his pride and write to his wife for funds to return to her.

No longer could he find justification for his lifestyle in the slight change he had been amused to make by removing the letter "g" from the Latin conclusion reached by the French philosopher Descartes: *Cogito ergo sum* (I think, therefore I am). No longer could Luigi find satisfaction in the linkage of his existence with his ability to copulate.

CHAPTER 15

Maria managed to make ends meet with the wages she received for preparing and serving food, and often cleaning up in the kitchen, at the Lorentti's cafe. Young Paul stayed with her at the cafe while Rosa attended parochial school and was cared for by the nuns after school hours until Maria could take her home for supper. In the evenings Maria busied herself with sewing, mending and the dozen other mind-numbing chores that needed to be done by a single parent in the early nineteen-twenties. Regardless of how tired she might be, however, she always managed to set aside at least an hour of quality time to be shared with her children. She read from the Bible her mother had given her (the 23rd Psalm and Luke 6:38 were favorites) and at the request of her children she read and re-read selected portions of Luigi's letters. The children's need for their papa grew with the passage of time, while Maria's conscious need for her husband diminished.

She still missed him though, especially at bedtime when she ached for his presence. The blue sensuality of Chicago style jazz, transported from the brothels of New Orleans to the speakeasies up north, moved through the wind-up Victrola's black megaphone into her viscera. Although Maria was unaware that jazz was originally spelled *jass* and was used as a slang expression for sexual intercourse, she could sense her husband's presence and longed for the feel of him when the pure tones of "Bix" Beiderbecke's *Way Down Yonder in New Orleans* spun off the thick black records into her darkened bedroom. Sometimes, after pouring herself a second glass of table wine, she got up and danced around the room pretending to hold her missing husband in her arms, then fell into bed and pretended to make love with him. These memory-borne fantasies appeared less frequently, victims of the demands on Maria's time made by running a house and raising children, but somehow retained their intensity as the physical separation of the couple stretched out to months and then years.

Their written correspondence declined in volume until one party wrote only in response to a letter received from the other one. At the same time, their letters reflected a qualitative loss of spontaneity, the fresh breath of true love. The soft unaffected words of affection became increasingly forced, hardened by the short-circuiting of true feelings by the contrived fabrications of the mind, and were hurtful. Did "absence make the heart grow fonder?" or did "out of sight, out of mind" apply to them?

One night Maria tried to restore the old feeling as she peered into her medicine cabinet mirror. At thirty-two years of age, was she still attractive? Would Luigi still love her? Are those tiny lines at the corner of her big almond eyes getting larger, her thick hair growing thinner? She took her hairbrush in hand and was reassured.

On the following morning, as if summoned by her desire, she received a letter from Luigi saying that he intended to rejoin his family in the near future. Maria's initial thrill was chilled by what came next. Unfortunately, the depression in Italy had hit the citizens of Torino and Milano the hardest, Luigi wrote, mainly because of the way the government in Rome sucked the financial blood out of the industrial North to finance politically beneficial development programs in the underdeveloped South. In the final paragraph came what a queasy feeling in her stomach had forewarned Maria to expect: Could Maria see her way clear to send her husband the equivalent of US$ 175 to pay for his ticket? With eternal love to you and the children, et cetera, et cetera.

Maria first counted up her liquid assets. She retrieved $98 hidden away under her mattress and emptied an additional $2.25 in small change from Rosa's piggy bank. She knew she could borrow the balance from the Lorentti's, which she did the following day. Maria then mailed the funds to Luigi and hoped with a kiss on her good luck coin and another on the envelope that the money would bring him home. Working against this hope there crawled deep inside her a persistent worm of doubt that went beyond a mere feeling to intuitive knowledge. Somehow, she *knew* that her man would use the money to pay for his unwholesome addictions.

Luigi persuaded the National (shipping) Line of Italy in Genova to issue him a free 1st class ticket in exchange for his entertaining the upper crust passengers on the liner *La Savoie*. The money provided by Maria was lost in card games with some low life cronies he had fallen in with during the crossing.

Maria knew she would be hard put to repay the Lorenttis' loan and asked them for advice on how she might raise the money. This discussion led Maria into an activity that some of her friends at church had found rewarding, but always spoke about in whispers, since the home production of wine and spirits was illegal and carried the risk of a jail sentence. Worse, the activity could risk trouble with the feared Sicilian *Mafia*, known locally as *La Mano Nera* (the Black Hand), whose operations had spread out in waves carried by the currents of illegal booze created by Prohibition from Chicago all the way to Spring Valley and the neighboring coal belt communities. The thought of supplementing her wages with the home production of wine was not new to Maria Suardi. When she had first dug into the backyard to plant a vegetable garden, maria's spade had struck a "tina," a vat used in making wine in a volume far exceeding household needs. Encouraged by the Lorentti's, and assisted by Anton Mandella, an aged next door neighbor skilled in the production of wine outside the purview of the law, Maria became a bootlegger.

Within a few days local Piemontesi arrived at night with 22-pound boxes of grapes from vineyards in California used to produce Grignolino, a dry, light-bodied red wine originally produced in small vineyards in the Alpine foothills of northern Italy. After the grapes were dumped into the tina, they were crushed under the white boots of the men who had delivered them to begin the production. As the volume increased, Anton suggested to Maria that she get in touch with the most prosperous and knowledgeable bootlegger in town, a skilled stonemason named Marcello Toffolo. This handsome northern Italian had gained a reputation among the local cognoscenti for the unusually smooth quality of the grappa he made and sold at considerable profit. While Maria learned that the really big money was in the sale of the distilled product of the grape, she was generally satisfied with the return from the sale of wine in her home.

At her behest, Maria was introduced to Toffolo by Grande at a church social. As soon as she could take him aside, Maria explained quite honestly her need for his help. Marcello was completely taken by the beauty, candor and self-reliance of the woman and immediately fell in love with her. Maria invited Marcello to her home the next evening and they discussed details of her new "business," after which they toasted their friendship. Maria put a record on the Victrola and they danced to the applause of the children, who liked the nice man, as did Maria.

During the following week, Maria and Rosa put up four dozen Mason jars of tomatoes, which served to camouflage the grappa cache, stored in a concrete vault built by Marcello. Access to the White Mule, as the drink was dubbed for its heavy kick, was provided by a small rubber tube hidden behind the tomato jars.

Marcello Toffolo was as much artist as mason, and he had gained considerable notoriety for his skill in applying different colored glazes to pottery and ceramic tiles. Best of all, this work, which he did in his spare time, was truly a labor of love.

He fondled each ceramic tile with the gentle love he felt for this beautiful woman whom God had brought into his life. Marcello was as shy as he was artistic, and try as he might, he was unable to hit on a way of communicating his love to its object. Finally, he decided to ask Maria to bring out her Tarot cards, in which the neighbors said she could divine the hidden meanings of past events and what the future might bring. (He did not know that Maria usually charged a dollar for each reading.) Perhaps these magical cards that were supposed to combine the Hebrew wisdom of the Kabbalha with the mystic sciences of ancient Egypt could expose the secret yearnings that he felt but could not bring himself to reveal.

After putting the children to bed, Maria brought forth the cards and placed the large deck on the dining table beside her Bible. Maria knew that the Church officially denied all forms of magic, but like other female magi (magicians) of which there was one in every Italian-American community, she also knew that her Church was too wise to actively oppose such popular occult practices. In any case, Maria regarded her Church and its parish activities, which were a living, breathing part of her family, as of far greater importance than the Church as a citadel of religious dogma and papal edicts. Therefore, she felt it perfectly appropriate to integrate the insights of the Tarot into the truths of the Bible. As was her custom, Maria laid her hand on the hand of Marcello and prayed for divine guidance before laying out the Tarot cards.

Marcello drank in the beauty of this woman, the highlights of her thick hair, high cheekbones and full lips accentuated by the flickering candle's light, and was unable to concentrate on the cards being placed on the table, or even to hear Maria's voice softly explaining their significance as she carefully laid them out in the shape of a cross. Marcello was hardly able to follow Maria's instructions to shuffle and to cut the cards into three piles as she moved through the procedures of the ancient Celtic method of Tarot reading. As she turned up the Ninth Card, signifying the subject's own hopes, Maria looked up into Marcello's eyes, a gentle smile appeared on her lips and a slight blush moved from her cheeks to her forehead. The card, placed next to the top of a four-card scepter beside the six-card cross formation, was Key VI – The Lovers – which depicted a naked Adam looking at an equally unclad Eve, both of them looking upwards at the Angel Raphael.

Maria cleared her throat and explained "Here is the attraction, beauty, harmony of the inner and outer life.

The power of choice means responsibility." Marcello nodded to acknowledge his understanding and eager acceptance of the wisdom of the Tarot.

The couple embraced, knowing with as much certainty as a human being can ever know that somehow, at some time their lives would be joined in holy matrimony.

At just that magic moment, the telephone jangled. Maria lifted the receiver from its cradle with a trembling hand, wondering who could possibly be calling at this late hour.

"Please forgive me, Marcello, but I must go out."

"But, why, my dear Maria?"

"It's the young immigrant girl down the street. She is having great difficulty delivering her baby. I must go. You understand." With a sweep of her hand, maria draped her shawl over her shoulders and took Marcello's hand. "Please stay here with my children. I'll return as soon as I can."

Toffolo nodded with a smile, and Maria Suardi went to perform what had become a routine duty. She could never remember exactly how or when she was taught the particular skill that often spelled the difference between life and death in the little homes of Spring Valley. She knew only that her neighbors depended on her assistance as an unlicensed but highly skilled midwife, and for Maria their deep gratitude was the only payment she received or sought.

When she returned home it was nearly three o'clock in the morning. The children were safe and sound. Marcello stayed through the night.

CHAPTER 16

Half way through a devil-may-care decade of exuberance that came to be known as the *Roaring Twenties*, Maria found herself caught up in the exciting currents of change that lifted women from positions of degrading inferiority to the sunny heights of proud achievement. The elevating power of the era was only strengthened by its incongruities: the classic, cool-eyed beauty of Greta Garbo awakened a longing among moviegoers that Lillian Gish and Mary Pickford had never captured; Gertrude Ederle, the first woman to swim across the English Channel, accomplished the feat in 14 hours, 31 minutes, nearly two hours faster than the time of the closest male swimmer; and Miriam "Ma" Ferguson became the first woman to be elected as a state governor by campaigning on the slogan "Me for Ma" in the traditionally male-dominated state of Texas.

Maria Suardi got into politics because she felt too

deeply about the welfare of her children to remain aloof. Again, she turned to Grande Lorentti for advice.

"Grande, I know you feel that it might be stupid, even dangerous, for me to get into politics."

"That is true, my dear Maria. It's a dog-eat-dog business, and I'm afraid that especially because you make the wine, you know, which is technically illegal – a crime – you may be vulnerable to pressure, extortion by the big boys in the smoke-filled backrooms."

"My dear Grande," said Maria to end the argument in a manner both friendly and decisive, "I really don't understand your big words, but I know you mean to protect me from harm, and for that I thank you from the bottom of my heart. But, listen, for the sake of my children and for the good of the community in which we live, I have no choice in the matter." Maria kissed her benefactor on the cheek, and continued. "Now, which of the candidates in next month's elections should I help?"

"Very well, Maria, but don't say I didn't warn you about getting into this dirty business. I personally am working, behind the scenes, for the election of an honest young lawyer named Edward M. Bingham, who is the Republican Party candidate to be judge of the Circuit Court. I have to caution you, however, that the judge he seeks to replace has powerful backers, including members of the Black Hand, the Mafia organization in Chicago."

"I'll work for Mr. Bingham," said Maria. And she did. Maria used her popularity among the Piemontesi miners, most of whom held to the anti-capitalist tenets of anarcho-syndicalism, to get them to vote for the young challenger. At first reluctant to vote at all, many of the miners had to be driven to the polls by Maria in her Model A Ford. After winning by the slim margin of a few hundred votes, Ed Bingham expressed his debt of gratitude to his benefactor and asked if there were any way he could repay her.

"Thank you, but there's nothing," she responded, adding, with a smile, "not right now in any case."

The mobsters backing the defeated judge were less than gracious, and were quick to repay Maria for her work. Within a few weeks, they blocked shipment from California of the grapes which Maria and other paesani depended on for the production of their wine. Maria refused to be intimidated. After hurried consultations with her fellow vintners, she collected their investment capital and rattled off in her Ford to the Chicago switch-yards.

During the trip north, Maria's extra-sensory perception reappeared to head off what could have been a perilous situation. Paul seemed to be taking a nap as he lay on the back seat two hours north of Spring Valley when suddenly Maria saw the shadow of the Grim Reaper move across the rear-view mirror. She instantly swerved into the driveway of a farmhouse, slammed on the emergency hand brake and pulled Paul out onto the ground. After inhaling carbon monoxide exhaust fumes that had leaked up into the back of the car, Paul was scarcely breathing and as pale as death itself. Maria dashed onto the steps of the farm house and, ignoring the old woman with the startled look who appeared in the doorway, grabbed a kerosene lamp mounted on the wall by the door and carried it to her son. In a single motion, Maria flung off the lamp's chimney and poured its fuel straight into Paul's mouth. He immediately vomited, choked and coughed but survived the poisonous fumes thanks to the action of a mother who was able somehow to perceive more than what was visible to her naked eye.

"*Grazie a Dio,*" whispered Maria as she crossed herself while holding her son tightly with one arm, "*Grazie a Dio.*"

At midnight, Maria made contact with a Milanese

forwarding agent who had no love for the Sicilian racke-
teers who handled most of the commodities shipped
through the Chicago rail hub. She handed over cash payment for the carload of grapes that four nights later
would be hurriedly unloaded at a siding behind
Marcello Toffolo's house.

Late that night, after a joyful party of Piemontese
vintners capped by a romantic interlude with Marcello,
Maria took the church calendar from her nightstand
drawer. The crossed dates covered nearly two pages
since Luigi was to have come home. Five weeks had
passed since Maria had inquired after her husband's
whereabouts at the shipping line's office in New York,
only to be told that he was last seen heading off to Boston
in the company of some gambler cronies. Maria was consumed by an anger so hot that it burned itself out in a
few days, replaced by sorrow and the inescapable realization that, for the childrens' sake, she would have to
clear the way for a new life – without Luigi.

After her rage subsided, Maria moved with cool
deliberation. She called on the town's only female attorney, Florence Salaroglio, and filed for divorce on grounds
of desertion. The year that she had to wait was the
longest year in Maria's young life. Each passing day
stretched out like overcooked pasta until she could
achieve the liberation of sleep at the outer limits of physical exhaustion reached by the fabrication of a dozen
trivial tasks to be performed after her kitchen work at the
Lorenttis' cafe, which, by itself, would have exhausted a
woman of less strength. *Maria Bella*, Beautiful Maria, as
she had come to be known, ironed Rosa's blouses, knit
winter sweaters and scarves for both children in the heat
of the summer with the time-saving efficiency of the
choppy, left-handed European strokes, and when all
other work was completed, moved into the alley to clean
the seats and scour the floorboards on her Model A.

Maria's only relief from her self-imposed drudgery came on weekends, when she could be together with Marcello, who now occupied a central position alongside her much-loved children. He was a man whose muscled arms could lift 100 kilos of solid granite without effort, but whose hands were as sensitive as the fingers of Pablo Cassals. The recollection of moments shared with the master stonemason, whose artistry as a glazier was well-known and sought out by the finest architects in the coal belt, nourished Maria with the warming pleasures of both recall and anticipation.

Maria knew Marcello Toffolo, who was fourteen years her senior, as a man of artistic mien, as a man of sensibility and gentle manners, and not least of all, as a man. A year was forever in terms of maintaining a loving relationship such as theirs without physical consummation of their shared desire. Maria knew this burning reality as well as her man and also understood that she must somehow keep the embers glowing at a point between a conflagration that would consume them with religious damnation and personal guilt, and the extinguishing of the physical fires of their emotions. This was, she knew, a difficult task – a task which Genesis as well as Schopenhauer, one of the philosophers with whom she had become acquainted through her library reading – considered, very simply, impossible. Yet, somehow Maria accomplished the task. She did so by planning activities shared with the children as the focal point: walks in the park, picking mushrooms, boiling them and testing for poison by dipping a silver coin in the water (if it turned black the batch was thrown out), rowing on the river and card games at home. And when she sensed that the embers were beginning to fade, she would manage to spend some quiet time alone with Marcello in the living room. And always, before she let him go, Maria hugged her man and whispered into his ear, "Please be patient,

Marcello, and remember: I love you."

As much as Maria enjoyed occasional intimacies with Marcello, the recollection of more intense and fulfilling pleasures of sensual encounters with Luigi kept appearing in her mind's eye. These uninvited images from the deep recesses of her subconscious appeared wherever she touched her hair brush or Roman coin, and served as constant reminders of her need to have Luigi Suardi in her life.

Shortly after her divorce was granted, Maria was married to Marcello in the City hall. She would have much preferred a church wedding, but she knew and accepted her Church's rule against church weddings for divorced persons. At a reception at the Lorenttis', which was planned as a small affair, more than a hundred of the couple's friends showed up, including a dozen miners scrubbed up for the occasion almost beyond recognition. Maria danced with all of them. Marcello beamed as he watched the uninhibited grace and energy of his young wife as she moved across the candlelit backyard in her bare feet, dancing to the music of a clarinet, mandolin and accordion played by professional musicians donating their talents as a wedding gift to the enormously popular couple.

After a short but immensely happy honeymoon visit to the Palmer House Hotel in Chicago, arranged by a branch office of the GOP in the Windy City, the Toffolos settled into a routine that, for the first time in a decade, provided Maria with some leisure hours to listen to phonograph records of the great Italian opera tenors and to read classical writings, of which she most enjoyed the works of Dante and the memoirs of Benvenuto Cellini.

Maria's life was not, however, to be devoid of excitement. Before moving into Toffolo's house, Maria was faced with the problem of what to do with the income producing wet goods stored in the cellar of her house.

"We could just leave the beverages where they are," suggested Marcello with a half-smile, knowing full well that his bride was not about to go along with the idea.

"You must have been drinking too much of the juice yourself, this very evening," said Maria, adding: "What would happen, do you think, if the new tenants discover the stores, as they surely will, and report us to the police?"

"Yes, you're quite right. But where shall we move it?"

"You know that old hotel just a couple of blocks away on Spalding Street that's been up for sale for months?"

"You mean that hot-sheet hotel, where they rent out rooms by the hour?"

"Yes, well, I don't know about that," said Maria blushing, "but do you think the owner might be willing to give us a six-months' lease on the property?"

"Possible," said Marcello, with a wink and a nod of his head. "I'll give the agent a call first thing in the morning. "You are a clever little girl," said Marcello and he gave his wife an appreciative hug.

On the next moonless night, a caravan of Piemontese friends transported several dozen bottles of Maria's finest wine and Toffolo's best grappa to their new storage site.

After Maria and her children moved into their new home, it was decided to lease the house on Seventh Street through a real estate agency. The rental income was kept in a special account with most of it used to pre-pay the mortgage, which Maria calculated would save thousands of dollars of interest payments.

The lessee was an out-of-town man named Pirelli, who dressed in fancy clothes, drove an English sports car and gave his occupation as "manufacturer's representative." The man mailed his monthly rental payments to Maria at least ten days before the end of each month until the Wall Street crash on Black Monday (October

24th) passed without the usual payment. In early November, Maria was concerned enough to ask her husband to call on Mr. Pirelli in person since the man never answered his telephone. Marcello was working almost around the clock on a large masonry contract and suggested that Paul be sent on the errand.

"But he's still so young," argued Maria.

"For a boy of ten, going on eleven, I'd say he's a very mature young man, my dear. I mean. look at the way he collects payments for the newspaper. Never a problem"

It was true, Paul had never had any difficulty with delivery of the evening paper, the *Moon Journal*, or collecting the $1.40 monthly payment from subscribers, including those who sometimes pretended to be out of the house when he rang their doorbells. ("But you didn't have to be Sherlock Holmes to see them peeking out from behind their curtain as I walked away," Paul once commented.)

"I think that being able to deal with strangers in a face-to-face situation like this is a very educational experience for a young man. Why, I never had to collect a bill from a stranger and just look at me: so bashful with strangers that I get all tongue-tied and red-faced when I have to deal with anyone I haven't known for a coon's age."

"Oh, my great big bashful beau, I like you just the way you are," said Maria as she gave her husband a hug. "But I guess you're right. It's just that he's growing up so fast, I always seem to be a year or two behind."

On the next Saturday, after completing his newspaper collection rounds, Paul was sent to the bungalow on Seventh Street to collect the rent. When he returned, Paul could hardly wait to tell his mother about the nice lady living there who had given him an envelope with the month's rent payment in cash.

"Not only that, Mama, but guess what?"

"What, son?"

"Well, this fine lady who rents our house was all dressed up in a sort of bathrobe that looked more like an evening gown, all shiny and covered with designs of birds and dragons and stuff."

"You don't say? Tell me more."

"Well, she had bright red lips and cheeks as rosy as Macintosh apples, and she smelled sweeter than anything. She gave me a Coke and an oatmeal cookie, too."

"She did? And then ..."

"Well, out of the back room came another nice lady in a bathrobe, and she smelled good, too. She patted me on top of the head and gave me a nickel to buy some candy. Wasn't that something?"

"It certainly was, Paul. But I have a feeling that those ladies living in our old house are up to no good, and I'm going to ask you never to go there again."

"Aw, but Mama," whined Paul.

"Never mind, just do as I say, said Maria sternly as she pretended to go for the little black umbrella standing in the corner, which both children recognized as more than a harmless symbol of her authority.

"Sure, Mama, I'll never go back there again."

"Thank you, Paul," said Maria and gave her son a big hug, the constant companion of the strict discipline administered by the lady with the help of her little black umbrella. After the children had gone to bed, Maria poured wine and silently waited. When Marcello put down his newspaper he looked into a face of cold anger he had never before seen, and would never forget. Her green eyes were turned grey; her voice was steely. "You will never again send Paul to that house." Marcello nodded quietly. "Never, ever again," said Maria and went to bed herself.

CHAPTER 17

The Great Depression of the thirties swept through the valley like a cloud as thick and black as the coal dust worn on the faces and engraved on the lungs of the miners who labored there. The carefree spirit of the twenties, encased in the seemingly indestructible music of the dance hall jazz bands and the high-kicking, short-skirted Charleston dancers, was suddenly, inexplicably replaced by the gloom of an overpowering need to survive. The economic collapse, which carried the threat of total ruin to many, somehow served to bring out the best, and sometimes the worst, in the people whose lives were most immediately threatened.

Maria, whose non-taxable income from bootleg wine and grappa sales had been wiped out by the repeal of Prohibition was in particularly dire straits. First, she called in her favor to Judge Bingham, asking him to give a job to Rosa, who had learned bookkeeping, typing and shorthand in high school and polished these skills in a secretarial school. In the evenings, Rosa helped her mother bake cookies, which were delivered by Paul after he completed his newspaper rounds to ladies in the church circle with the money to pay for them.

Neither of her children was told that the recipients of the baked goods paid for them. Instead, the the kids were led to believe that their work, which Paul regarded as fun, was simply an act of friendship and Christian charity for the benefit of friends of the family.

In the same vein, Paul was encouraged to set up a stand in front of the house to sell vegetables that Maria raised in a small garden in the Lorenttis' large backyard. Again, he saw this activity as great fun, a sort of make-believe business game much like the way younger kids sold lemonade at roadside stands in the summertime. His many customers, who were aware of the family's need for money, never let on that their purchases were anything but a part of Paul's little game.

Thanks to her political contacts in both parties, Maria got the job of distributing relief supplies to families in her precinct for which she received cash payment. She also had the benefit of storing, in the basement, canned goods, rice and beans earmarked for relief. Occasionally, some of this food would appear on the Toffolo dinner table. No questions were ever asked where it came from.

In the latter part of the thirties Maria, preoccupied as she was with the need to save money for Paul's college, had nearly put Luigi out of her thoughts when the parcel arrived. It was addressed to Paul and bore a Boston postmark. Inside was a brand new accordion with Paul's name engraved on a chrome plate on the top. Paul was ecstatic, and Maria fled to her bedroom to conceal her tears of mixed sadness and joy from her son.

Within a year, Paul had learned to play the instrument so well that Maria arranged for him to give a recital at the Lorenttis.

"Oh, Mama, that will be nice. But I wonder, do you suppose ..."

"Do I suppose what, son."

"Do you suppose I could invite my father to come and listen to me play. Would that be all right?"

"I suppose so," said Maria, who quickly went into the kitchen to attend to some urgent task, her heart beating so loudly she feared her son might hear the sound.

The recital was held in the Lorenttis' parlor. There were a dozen invited guests in attendance and one invited guest hidden in the hydrangea shrubbery outside the open parlor window. Luigi had been elated by the invitation Paul sent him. The prospect of seeing his son and his beloved Maria kept Luigi from getting a good night's sleep for more than a week. Finally, he had to bite the bittersweet bullet and buy "a railroad ticket into my past, and, who knows, maybe into my future as well," he mused as he considered the meaning of the trip.

When he arrived at the Lorenttis', Luigi's resolve evaporated and his feet froze, unable to proceed up the steps of the porch. Concealed in the bushes, he rationalized, "I'll just wait until the end of the recital." But the concert took an unexpected turn.

In the anticipation that his father would be present, Paul chose a program of sentimental favorites starting with the lively *Tic-Toc Polka* ("Tic tic tic toc goes my heart with the clock. Don't they know I am dancing with you ..."). Then came a song newly published in Milano which brought tears to Maria's eyes: *Mam ma so-lo per te la mia can-zo ne vo-la* ("Mama, it's just for you this little song I'm singing"). Next came a number whose lyrics cut straight through all of Maria's protective scar tissue, *Non ti scordar di me* ("Say you will not forget"). Maria had to sob openly when Paul played and sang "My life is linked with yours, since that sweet moment when we met." Then when he concluded his recital with *Maria, Mari!* it was too much for his mother to bear.

"Stop!" she commanded through her tears. Paul, please forgive me. Your playing is so beautiful. And I'm sorry, but I have to return the accordion to your father." A hush fell over the guests, and Maria explained, "I cannot let my son grow up to be like ..." Unable to finish her sentence, and filled with remorse, Maria ran from the house in pursuit of the man whom she knew had been concealed in the bushes, the love of her life.

The two were reunited at last at the entrance to the hotel where Luigi had booked a room. The night clerk stood up from his swivel chair behind the counter, but before he could recite the rule against female visitors in the rooms of male guests, Luigi pushed a dollar bill across the counter and said, "It's all right. We are married."

The inhibitions imposed by guilt fell with their clothing and the lovers worshiped at the temples of their bodies without the intrusion of words or thoughts. Her eyes were opened by a shaft of light that peered through a tear in the curtain. Maria got dressed and looked down into the smiling eyes of Luigi, who said, "I'm going to get a job in Chicago, Maria. We'll be able to see ..." Maria nodded, laid her hand softly on Luigi's lips and smiled, whispered into his ear "arriverderci," and left.

Marcello, who had recognized Luigi and knew in his sorrow that Maria was with him, sat on the porch in the light of the moon until Maria appeared at sunrise walking across the field. All she could say was, "I'm sorry." Marcello nodded and silently went to bed. Maria slept on the sofa in the living room, and never heard Marcello leave for his new job at the stone quarry. It was a job for which he had little training and less interest, but the decline in new housing starts had virtually eliminated the need for masons, and he was too proud to go on the dole or otherwise fail to pull his weight in keeping the household afloat.

The sound was muffled, but any explosion in the Valley caused the inhabitants to stop in their tracks and shiver with the recollection of the explosion in the pits that had trapped scores of miners and cost a dozen lives a few years earlier. News quickly spread that the guttural sound had come from the quarry across the river. A worker had accidentally been killed. According to the report of the mine superintendent carried in the paper that evening, the victim of the blast was a new man assigned to help the blaster reduce huge Dolemitic limestone boulders into pieces that would fit into the plant's crusher. The novice had cut ten fuse cords in one-foot lengths, which would burn down in a minute, and put them on top of a row of ten stones. He then inserted the highly unstable dynamite made of nitro-glycerin used in those days into holes drilled in the center of the stones. The fuses were then put into the dynamite and lighted, one after the other. The rocks blew in sequence, and the blaster counted them. After the ninth explosion the new man, identified as a mason named Toffolo, emerged from cover, the blaster shouted for him to get back, that only nine charges had gone off, but it was too late.

Maria was stricken with consuming guilt and wore mourning black for the next year and a half. The only thing that took her mind from her guilt-ridden grief was her dedicated effort to get Paul into college. The half o f the thousand dollar life insurance money left over after Marcello's burial under a marble headstone, was put in a savings account that earned 1.5% interest. Another thousand dollars in small bills were found concealed in a little safe depository Marcello had fashioned behind a stone in the basement that had supported the old grappa still. The fact that her late husband had never told Maria about this cache served to relieve Maria of some of her guilt, and she shed her black clothes in favor of the bright

colors for which she had become famous among the
townspeople.

❖❖❖

In the summer of 1937, Maria drove to the
University of Illinois campus to interview a former
neighbor, Mrs. Balistrire, to ascertain if her boarding
house was good enough for Paul. The cuisine, northern
Italian, passed her inspection. When Maria was told that
all of the boarders were from Italian Catholic families,
she signed a contract, returned home and told Paul to
pack his bags. Mindful of his mother's tight financial circumstances, Paul offered to stay home and get a job to
help out for a year. Maria was adamant, however, that
education came first. So Paul left home, first to study in
college and then to fight in the war against the Axis pow-
ers: Nazi Germany and, ironically, the homeland of both
his parents.

In the spring of 1945, Maria was 53 years old and still
a beauty as she sat on a throne atop the Grand Marshal's
float in a parade to celebrate Columbus Day. Halfway
down Main Street, Maria shouted with joy as she spotted
her son in the crowd, wearing the uniform of an Army
Captain. He saluted her, and she motioned for him to
climb up on the float. Less than a minute later, they both
saw him at the same time, and screamed aloud. How had
he gotten there? No time for questions. Paul jumped
down and lifted his father up onto the float. The
bystanders cheered and applauded as one. The reunited
family embraced each other like long-lost friends, which,
in a way, they were. Near the end of the parade route, a
beautiful young lady called out to Maria.

"Maria bella, I'm going to be engaged to be married
and I want you to do me a favor."

"Certainly, my dear girl, what is it?"

"Could you please read my fortune for me?"

"Of course, come along with us to my house."

Maria poured out wine and served a plate of cookies for her guests before disappearing into the kitchen to get her Tarot cards. Maria appeared surprised and happy to find that the cards promised the young lady a bright future and a happy marriage. "Are you sure," asked the bride-to-be.

"Absolutely, my dear. The cards never lie." Whereupon her new friend gave Maria a hug of thanks and danced from the house with a smile that went from ear to ear and shone like the sun.

"Maria" said Luigi, as he raised his glass in salute, "you fixed those cards, didn't you?"

"No, my friend, never," said Maria in a tone of outraged innocence.

"Mother," said Paul with a raised eyebrow.

"Well, maybe just a little," said Maria, as she raised her glass to conceal a big smile.

Luigi took a sip of wine, chuckled and shook his head. "My beautiful Maria. You're so Italian."

"Look who's talking," she said, "and why would we ever want to be anything else?"

ORDER FORM

Please send _____ copy/copies of **Maria Bella** to:

Name _____

Address _____

City _____

State, Zip _____

Telephone (optional) _____

Price:	$10.00 per copy*	$ _____
Shipping:	$3.00 for the first and $2.00 for each additional book	$ _____
Sales Tax:	Add 5.6% for shipment to Wisconsin addresses	$ _____
	TOTAL	$ _____

Kindly enclose a check with your order
(we're too small to handle plastic) and mail to:

Thistlefield Studio
7434 Carter Circle N.
Franklin, WI 53132

Quantity Purchases

For discount prices on the purchase and shipping of
two or more copies, please call us at:

1-800-968-1294